FROM SOCIAL COMPETITION TO SOCIAL DUMPING

Social Europe Series, Volume 35

FROM SOCIAL COMPETITION TO SOCIAL DUMPING

Edited by

Jan Buelens
Marc Rigaux

intersentia
Cambridge – Antwerp – Portland

Intersentia Ltd
Sheraton House | Castle Park
Cambridge | CB3 0AX | United Kingdom
Tel.: +44 1223 370 170 | Fax: +44 1223 370 169
Email: mail@intersentia.co.uk
www.intersentia.com | www.intersentia.co.uk

Distribution for the UK and Ireland:
NBN International
Airport Business Centre, 10 Thornbury Road
Plymouth, PL6 7 PP
United Kingdom
Tel.: +44 1752 202 301 | Fax: +44 1752 202 331
Email: orders@nbninternational.com

Distribution for Europe and all other countries:
Intersentia Publishing nv
Groenstraat 31
2640 Mortsel
Belgium
Tel.: +32 3 680 15 50 | Fax: +32 3 658 71 21
Email: mail@intersentia.be

Distribution for the USA and Canada:
International Specialized Book Services
920 NE 58th Ave. Suite 300
Portland, OR 97213
USA
Tel.: +1 800 944 6190 (toll free) | Fax: +1 503 280 8832
Email: info@isbs.com

ISBN 978-1-78068-352-2
D/2016/7849/47
NUR 825

British Library Cataloguing in Publication Data. A catalogue record for this book is available from the British Library.

PREFACE

"From Social Competition to Social Dumping" is the title of the collection of papers written on the occasion of the symposium which took place in Antwerp on 20 and 21 November 2014. In this book the phenomenon of social dumping is looked at in the wider context of the liberalized social competition as steered by the European Union. Special attention is paid to the harrowing dumping practices in the road transport sector. Therefore this publication contains a number of testimonies by people who actively fight social dumping. Some of the authors also examine the phenomenon of social dumping in relation to compliance with every worker's fundamental right to respect for his/her dignity as a human being. In this respect, the underlying question is whether, by tolerating legislation that allows human dignity to be violated by social dumping, the European and national legislators do not infringe on the primary fundamental right...

Marc Rigaux
Jan Buelens

CONTENTS

PART I

CONTRIBUTIONS

CHAPTER 1
THE RIGHT TO HUMAN DIGNITY AT STAKE

Marc RIGAUX*

1. INTRODUCTION – A COMPLEX SOCIAL ISSUE SHAPED AND PROVOKED BY EUROPEAN LAW

As a result of the neoliberal philosophy and politics which inspired its conception and implementation, the economic unification of Europe has claimed a lot of victims. What is more, this neoliberalism continues to animate, without any inhibition whatsoever, the political, legislative and judicial initiatives of the European institutions. There can be no doubt that neoliberalism is the Union's official ideology. The realization of the single market has come about without any adjusting or accompanying economic and social policies. The effects of the establishment of the single market on social and human relations go far beyond the economic and commercial domains its authors had in mind. In fact, the single market has led to changes in European society that are so far-reaching that they could very well be qualified as mutations. They can be found at three levels: the primary economic level, the social level, and finally the general or societal level. At the primary economic level the establishment of the single market has given rise to increased, extensive and often harsh competition between the various economic actors, prompting the creation of bigger companies and frequently damaging the local economies and SMEs. Thus, the unification has produced a torrent of restructuring operations, in many cases resulting in a loss of jobs or in delocalization and transfers of jobs. The competitive violence to which European undertakings have been subjected has been reinforced by the Union's and the Member States' accession to the Free Trade Treaty that established the WTO. This accession has led to the globalization, in fact and in law, of certain markets, thus pushing the economic pressure on European entrepreneurs and employers to the limit. The Europeanization and globalization have come about without any major accompanying economic policies, resulting

* Emeritus Professor of Labour Law, University of Antwerp.

in the creation of an environment that is adverse to the reinforcement of the industry in Europe. Indeed, by choosing a largely monetary-oriented economic approach the European institutions have been contributing to the destabilization and weakening of the European economic actors... sometimes entailing a considerable increase in unemployment. The bank crisis has had a catalysing effect and has only reinforced the lack of adjusting economic policies. This is a failure which has resulted in social massacres in Spain, Greece and Portugal.

At the social level the outcome is hardly better and, if possible, even more of a mess. The establishment of the single market has led to the introduction of a transnational labour market, based on the free movement of workers and services and permanently freed of inconvenient national borders. Here too there is a serious lack of consistent social policies. The transnational labour market has substantially increased the social competition among salaried workers as well as between salaried workers and self-employed workers of the various Member States. It has also led to competition between national labour law and social law systems, a logical consequence of the distribution of competences between the European legislature and national legislature. So, the foundation of a single labour market has had devastating effects on the level and quality of employment, on the quality of pay and working conditions, and finally on the quality of social protection in general. Following this socially unadjusted unification of the labour market, the social exclusion at Union level has reached levels which are intolerable from a social point of view. The same goes for social exploitation. Certain sectors have been destroyed by aggressive practices of social dumping. Finally, to complete the picture we have to point out that the social dialogue is moribund. Although the failure of the neoliberal approach of the labour market is obvious, the European institutions cheerfully continue their policies of liberation of the labour market. The growing impoverishment of the European population does not seem to embarrass them at all.

The third and final level concerns a more general level and refers to society as a whole. The establishment of the internal market was accompanied by a revision and redefinition (largely implicitly) of the role of the State as an economic (and therefore social) actor. As part of an approach supported by all the European institutions, quite a lot of services and activities previously offered and organized by the public authorities have been privatized and made competitive.

The loss of economic influence of the State has reinforced its political impairment due to the transfer of power to the European legislature. But that is not all. The monetary policies of the European Central Bank, reinforced by the policies to expedite the recovery of the banking sector, have considerably contributed to the commodification of the State. The State has become a stock exchange product in which the market invests or disinvests. Politics are dominated by the market and the State loses its influence. This situation is not without consequences for the citizens' perception of national politics. They consider themselves to be (and are) subjected to national institutions which no longer seem to be able to deal efficiently with the social and economic difficulties the population faces. In fact, these institutions no longer have the room for manœuvre necessary to develop adequate political and economic strategies. Bound by budgetary restrictions, limited in their power to act as a result of the transfer of powers to the Union, these institutions seem defenceless and paralysed. So it is not unsurprising that part of the population has the impression that their national leaders are incompetent and disinterested. However, in fact, the ones responsible for the inaction are the European authorities, which, struck by a neoliberal paralysis, beatifically expect that the market will solve their economic and social problems. Moreover, those very same European authorities consider the high unemployment levels and the impoverishment of the people to be collateral damage of their neoliberal remedies for the crisis – in other words, a necessary evil until the budgetary severity, imposed in an authoritarian manner on the Member States will... not bear fruit. Needless to say, this approach has had a devastating effect on the attitude of European citizens. It is no surprise that faced with the degeneration of their national parliamentary systems citizens have been showing a growing indifference towards the European cause. The neoliberal European construction seems to have turned into a source of scission of society and of discord, a construction in which the democratic deficit keeps increasing. The Union is suffering from an identity and confidence crisis but the European institutions do not seem to be aware of this.

Law has always played an essential role in the European unification. The European Union is an extremely complex contractual construction. Based on very elaborate political compromises, the European institutions have considerable decision-making powers. However, despite the fact that a lot of competences, as well as part of their sovereignty, have been transferred from the Member States to the Union, the latter cannot claim the status of a State. Even though its powers have a legislative, judicial or administrative character, the Union continues to derive its primary legitimacy from conventions between the States. Thus, in essence, the initiative of the creators of the Union concerns a political action, directly and necessarily supported and united by law. Not only does the law make the unification possible and durable, it also attempts to prevent political conflicts between Member States. So the fundamental importance of the law for the European integration rests on its stabilizing and creative power. Another reason for emphasizing the law's essential role has to do with its binding capacity. The European Union imposes a binding economic order upon its Member States. This economic order has been laid down in a legal structure which dominates the national legal systems. The European Commission and the high European courts, appointed to make sure that the Member States respect the European economic order, have a number of adequate and formidable sanctions at their disposal. As a result of its dynamizing function, the law has helped to facilitate the integrating mission of the European Court of Justice. In part, European integration is founded on the case law of the Court. This means that the integration is not only based on legislative actions, but also on judicial steps which would be inconceivable without the valuable support of the law. These are three good reasons to state that the law not only shapes the European economic identity, but also supports, stimulates and provokes it, thus providing the economic order with a very solid institutional anchoring.

But which economic order does this actually concern; what are its foundations and what are its constitutive elements? Well, it concerns a neoliberal economic order ensuing from the capitalist market economy. Its foundations are the freedom of enterprise and the freedom of labour, market freedoms and free (social) competition. In addition, of course, we must not forget the right of private property. Since in the market economy a contract continues to be the instrument par excellence to regulate market relations, individual freedom of contract constitutes the cornerstone of the whole system. The freedom in question is a freedom in law, based on the equality in law of the citizens. Although the market economy has been in existence for several centuries, never before have the founding principles of liberalism been translated so faithfully in law than in the structures of the European Union. The right to free movement of capital, goods, services and workers has provided market freedom with the most solid legal anchoring ever since the moment these freedoms were raised to the level of fundamental economic rights. In the wake of the market freedoms, the right of free (social) competition is another legal pillar of the European liberal economic order. Finally, given that it is among the rights protected by the Charter of Human Rights of the European Union, the freedom of enterprise has also been elevated to the level of a fundamental right. The respect for the superiority of these market rights is essentially based on a double institutional blocking mechanism because both the European Commission and the European Court of Justice monitor this very closely and, in the event of non-compliance, impose severe sanctions.

Within the European construction the law constitutes a considerable federative element. Its action and importance far surpass its traditional functions. In fact, where, as a rule, the law determines and stabilizes social relations, European (economic) law for its part promotes and stimulates economic integration. The administrative practice of the Commission and the case law of the Court of Justice form the foundations of an integration that could be qualified as being of a judicial nature. Here more than elsewhere the law is a major factor in the formation of social relations. In our view this is particularly the case in terms of the liberalization of the labour market where the law (subject to sanctions of the Court of Justice) reinforces social competition, including certain social dumping practices.

2. THE FREE LABOUR MARKET AND FREE SOCIAL COMPETITION AS THE FOUNDATIONS OF LABOUR RELATIONS

2.1. FREE MARKET ECONOMY, FREE LABOUR MARKET AND FREE SOCIAL COMPETITION

2.1.1. Market economy as a reference system

The organization of labour relations is always grafted onto an underlying economic system. As a result the structures and methods of labour relations are in line with the main economic framework. Subsequently social, cultural and legal factors define the concrete shape and specifics of each system. Therefore, even though anchored in the same kind of capitalist economy the labour relations organized by law can differ per country, region or sector. However, and despite the differences, the social and legal regulations governing labour relations will yield to the requirements of the market economy. The leading principles of the economic system will be respected. In fact, they impose themselves, explicitly or tacitly, on the various social actors. Within the European Union the national legislations on labour relations have in common that they correct the free labour market and free social competition. Nonetheless, these laws are very different in terms of the degree and intensity of the social corrections, the importance of social dialogue as a source of regulations, or in terms of the room for manœuvre left to the courts. Still, all these legal systems, different as they may be, respect the freedom of labour, of enterprise and of social competition as the foundations of labour relations. With the intention of liberating the labour market, the European institutions' actions to stimulate integration have continuously and progressively reinforced the common economic and legal basis of these legislations at the expense of national legal provisions supporting social corrections.

2.1.2. The free labour market and the commercialization of labour

It is typical of the market economy that, a priori, all things and activities can be qualified as a commodity, susceptible to becoming the object of a commercial transaction. Usually commercialization refers to the fact that a thing or an activity becomes a product or commodity that can be sold on the market. As we will see later, even a right or a State can be commercialized. The market mechanism cannot do anything to curtail this process. Even a market gets merchandized as soon as it is faced with competition. In the past only political institutions at various levels made a reservation, inspired by economic, social, cultural, humanitarian motives or simply out of respect for human dignity. Now that we are confronted with globalized markets adequate political institutions are sorely lacking. The existing reservations to the commercialization relate almost exclusively to the national legislators and markets and do not in any way involve transnational practices. The feeling of powerlessness is made even bigger by the increasingly virtual nature of the markets which, for the most part, are made and unmade on the Internet. It is up to the politicians to regulate the functioning of the transnational markets, just as it is up to them to decide on the legitimate and (especially) illegitimate ways to make money. However, it seems that the (international) politicians have not taken in the full scale of the human damage caused by a market economy which is not only "planned" but above all used by private interest groups for their own benefit.

In view of the abovementioned observations, it will not be surprising that in a market economy labour (potential) is considered to be a commodity. It goes without saying that the market fixes the price (pay and working conditions) of labour. In order to avoid legal constructions in which a person would have the right to own another person, the civil legislator used a fictive operation. He made a separation between work and the person carrying out the work. Thus the way was paved for the conception of an employment contract, meaning that there were no longer situations in which a person could obtain the right to own another person, either partially or temporarily – situations that, unwittingly, evoke the spectre of slavery.

2.1.3. Labour as an object of social competition

For an overwhelming majority of people all over the world, finding a paid job continues to be a matter of life and death. By selling their labour potential they obtain the necessary means to provide for themselves. Without work they are condemned to a marginalized life. From a moral point of view, the social competition introduced by the free labour market should not be compared with other forms of economic competition because it is a matter of the very existence of man and his quality of life. It concerns – no more, no less – the dignity of man (at work). However, the economic reality is very different. The market economy, which has now become globalized, has "freed" itself from legal national obstacles and hardly bothers with moral observations. The manufacturers' search for cheap high-quality labour potential has created a downward spiral of social competition. The Europeanization and globalization of certain segments of the labour market have led to social competition in Europe and the rest of the world, in the context of which workers benefiting from consistent labour legislation enter into competition with workers who do not enjoy this kind of legislation. In other words, the costs of a paid worker, directly influenced by the (non-)existence of social legislation worth its name, constitute the main element of this transnational social competition. Needless to say that this process has a devastating effect on the level of protection and income of the workers, especially in the European Union. The degradation of labour and social law goes hand in hand with a loss of employment and of quality of employment, as well as with impoverishment and overall marginalization.

The constant decrease of the level of protection the less well-off have against the detrimental effects of the market economy in Europe has not been compensated for by an equivalent growth of social protection in other regions of the world. On the contrary, the unreserved domination of the market logic has only contributed to the division of society worldwide. The distance between the rich and the poor, between exploiters and the exploited, is becoming wider and wider. Parallel to the institutionalization of the market economy at the European and global level, neoliberal ideology has reached the status of a dogma, thus by definition not allowing any questioning of its scope or pertinence. Therefore, unlimited competition in terms of employment is not a secondary effect of the introduction of liberalized transnational markets; it is its main element and objective. As we will see later, the domination of the market threatens human dignity as well as the democratic fabric of society. Even more seriously, in the long term it will also threaten the very foundations of civilization.

2.1.4. Free social competition: concept, types and consequences

Social competition is understood to mean the competition between all those who are obliged to provide for themselves by selling their labour potential, i.e. by finding or keeping a paid job. This definition does not make any distinction between the positions the jobseekers may have. As a result, social competition governs wage and salaried workers as well as self-employed workers, civil servants, worker-owners and even moonlighters. Social competition presents itself in a direct or an indirect form. It may concern the internal or external labour market. It can be qualified as direct when it sets up jobseekers against each other within the same legal space. It is indirect when it concerns several legal spaces. A legal space is understood to mean a unity where the same legal rules apply. An undertaking, a sector, a State or even a continent can be legal spaces. In this line of thinking, social dumping would be an indirect form of social competition because it concerns at least two different legal spaces. The direct or indirect nature of the competition depends entirely on the group of persons or jobseekers concerned or targeted. Social competition will be fair or unfair depending on whether or not it respects the rules of competition law. Certain forms of unfair social competition amount to social exploitation, more specifically when they constitute a violation of the right to human dignity. As certain forms of social dumping manifestly violate human dignity at work, they can be qualified as social exploitation.

But what are the consequences of social competition? Social competition can lead to social exploitation if the conditions and circumstances violate the fundamental right of respect for human dignity. The obligation of respect for human dignity involves a relative aspect as well as an absolute or universal aspect. The relative aspect of the protection of human dignity refers to the specific legal space in which the constitutive elements of the violation occur. This means that it is possible that the wage system applied to the workers leaves much to be desired within a national or regional legal context but not so at the wider global level. The same applies to the system of working hours. The universal aspect on the other hand refers to elements that constitute infringements of human dignity in all legal spaces. This concerns in particular anything related to forced labour or child labour or even certain forms of discrimination in the workplace.

Social exclusion is another major consequence of social competition. The degree of employability of certain persons or certain groups can be so low that they do not or no longer succeed in getting hired. They are excluded, either temporarily or permanently. Social exclusion can occur on the internal labour market as well on the external one. If it occurs on the internal labour market, i.e. within an undertaking, it is called suspension of the contract in the case of temporary exclusion, and dismissal in the case of permanent exclusion.

Other consequences of social competition remain (a priori) outside the law. They concern the quality of the relations between workers and/or jobseekers. Excessive social competition or a form of social competition little or badly supported can considerably reduce a person's social resistance. At the collective level it can weaken the feeling of solidarity within the group to which the individual belongs. This should not be surprising since from a psychological point of view the competition scheme is a scheme of exclusion or (virtual) elimination of the person facing competition. The one who is best at competing eliminates the other. Social competition undermines good fellowship among workers and strengthens the attitude of everyone for themselves. In the long term social competition threatens the cohesion of the group and of society as a whole.

2.2. THE FREE LABOUR MARKET AND FREE SOCIAL COMPETITION: STRUCTURAL LEGAL ANCHORING

2.2.1. Free labour market and free social competition: cornerstones of a legal order

The law consists of rules of conduct emanating from society. These rules have binding power. Within societies legal orders have been established, i.e. a set of rules applicable to groups of persons, groups within which there are hierarchic or hierarchized relations. The legal order of the State is without a doubt the most important legal order in a nation. It is the backbone of society. Its norms represent the essence of the organization of society and of the State. As the State order emanates from the sovereign nation, which in its turn is the emanation of the will of the people, the State order claims the authority to judge the lawfulness of other legal orders. Indeed, there are numerous other legal orders. Some are readily subject to the State order and claim that by doing so they have the right to exist. Other orders on the other hand declare themselves to be autonomous without apparent links with the legal order of the State. But in reality there are power relations between these orders. Even though the State can invoke the dominance of its legal order over that of the others, this dominance still needs to be in line with the power relations of the other existing orders. If not, the State does not have the necessary power to impose its rules of conduct.

The rules of conduct governing the existence and functioning of the market economy constitute a legal order that is partly grafted on the legal order of the State. As a result there can be no doubt about the legitimacy of the capitalist legal order. It is a fact that it derives the legality of its existence and its functioning from the legal order of the State. However, in our view it is not all that certain that this declaration of legitimacy covers the entirety of the legal order. For instance, as regards the policy governing the labour market, certain practices of professional organizations seem to us difficult to reconcile with the Belgian constitutional order. The same goes for certain financial practices and stock exchange dealings that escape the political control of the States. Therefore (conformity) conflicts between legal orders cannot be excluded. The power relations between the conflicting orders decide which rules will be applied. The dominant legal system is the one that succeeds in enforcing compliance with its rules. In fact, the legal system of the free market often prevails over the order of the State because the latter hardly ever manages to prohibit the application of the rules and norms of the capitalist legal order. As far as labour relations are concerned, the free market and free social competition assert themselves as the leading principles. EU law on the freedoms of the market, reinforced by the international law on free trade, gives the economic order a solid legal anchoring.

2.2.2. Labour relations and free social competition: market relations and power relations

The term "labour relations" usually refers to the relations between employers and their employees. This presupposes the existence of a contractual bond between the employer and the worker he employs, i.e. an employment contract. By means of the employment contract the worker enters the undertaking. He/she leaves the external labour market to join the internal labour market, i.e. the undertaking. Given the fact that the organization of production requires planning, the internal labour market is a semi-planned market. As for social competition, which also occurs within an enterprise, this is now canalized and given a concrete form. So the organization of labour takes shape against a background of social competition. This means that the labour relations continue to be market relations between, on the one hand, the employer, expected to organize the internal labour market, and social competition (and the workers subject to social competition), on the other. Personnel management is the preferred instrument to organize this competition. As a result of their forced competition the workers become the subordinates of the owners of the undertaking who in fact are also the capital owners. The employer is the legal embodiment of the dominance of the capital owners. The workers are required to compete with each other within the undertaking. The legal structure of the undertaking reinforces their position of dependence by failing to create a legal tie between them. Only trade union freedom allows them to transcend the competitive relations and to form ties of professional solidarity.

2.2.3. *Structural anchoring in law*

The legal anchoring of the principles of the free market and free social competition has been established at various levels and in various forms. First, the anchoring came about tacitly and indirectly in national law. Indeed, Belgian law has never explicitly recognized the principle of the free market nor that of free social competition. By contrast it did guarantee other rights, necessary for the functioning of the market economy, such as the right to private property and the right to freedom of enterprise. Apparently the Belgian legislator also regulated certain commercial practices with the intention of protecting and preserving the well-functioning of the market, thus showing his commitment to the liberal economy and its foundations. It goes without saying that at present the most important part of this legal anchoring is to be found in European law. The law on the market freedoms and economic law definitely radiate approval of neoliberalism and the market economy. By its case law the European Court of Justice reinforces and legitimizes the preponderance of the market ideology over social relations in Europe.

3. FREE SOCIAL COMPETITION, SOCIAL EXPLOITATION AND SOCIAL EXCLUSION

3.1. SOCIAL EXPLOITATION AND SOCIAL EXCLUSION: INEVITABLE CONSEQUENCES OF FREE SOCIAL COMPETITION

Without social corrections the free labour market cannot but lead to social exploitation and exclusion, and this for two major reasons. The first has to do with the almost structural unbalance at a general level between supply and demand of employment. Although for certain segments of the labour market other relations between supply and demand are possible (and even likely), at the general level the demand greatly exceeds the supply of employment. Hence, there is a bad quality-price ratio for the jobseeker. The existence of free social competition works against him/her and pushes him/her into a negative spiral of social competition, directly leading to pitiful pay and working conditions. Besides, the same unbalance is also the main cause of the high degree of social exclusion. The second reason, of a completely different order, concerns the legal framework of the market. Making the individual, who has become a citizen, the nucleus of society is typical of the liberal conception of social relations. The citizen who is free and equal in law has autonomy of judgement and power of discernment, thus making him/her entirely responsible for his/her actions and choices. As a result of the refusal to take account of the economic inequality between citizens, those citizens are left to the mercy of the rules of the power relations when they have to negotiate about (employment) contracts. The fact that in terms of the economy they are forced to accept dubious working conditions does in no way detract from their responsibility. Indeed, by being free and equal in law "nothing" forces them to accept bad working conditions. Liberal contract law in no way puts a check on the negative social competition spiral. On the contrary, it provokes and reinforces it, even though this spiral leads directly to exploitation and exclusion. No doubt the beatitude of the liberal legislators can be explained by their unshakeable belief in the (long-term) beneficial effects of the functioning of the market. Even faced with the wide social divide the liberal legislators do not act or intervene. They simply wait until the market recovers, thus heading for disaster.

3.2. SOCIAL EXPLOITATION AND SOCIAL EXCLUSION: PROPOSAL OF TYPIFICATION

In earlier publications we tried to define the phenomenon of social exploitation in legal terms, starting from its principal characteristics. We chose to define it as follows: social exploitation is the sum of facts, actions and attitudes imputable to physical or legal persons, with the intention of profiting unlawfully from the economic dependence of another person in order to force him/her to work in circumstances and with pay and working conditions which are degrading from a human point of view and certainly contrary to respect for the rights that guarantee human dignity. The definition of the phenomenon, even somewhat individualized, should not make us forget that social exploitation is a practice with structural causes of a collective and universal character. Its causes are structural because they are directly linked to the functioning of the market economy, an economy that creates non-adjusted social competition, thus leading to the exploitation of the less well-off. Usually the exploitation also has a collective dimension because it has to operate on a general level to assume the durable character necessary for its existence. Social exploitation is universal because it is rooted in a globalized economy. On examining the phenomenon we find that there are a number of useful criteria for distinction, meaning that it would seem appropriate to distinguish between the different types of exploitation on the basis of the economic or legal space concerned, on the basis of the degree of complexity of the legal structures shaping the exploitation, or even on the basis of the gravity of the exploitation. Depending on the economic and legal space in question, social exploitation can be concentrated in a certain branch or affect a whole region, country, continent or even the whole world. Depending on the complexity of the structures used to organize the exploitation, these can be referred to as simple structures or complex ones. A situation in which the exploited worker is employed directly by the physical or legal person that exploits him/her could be qualified as simple. More complex, on the other hand, is the situation in which the exploitation is the product of inadequate functioning of the network companies. In this case, social exploitation is the direct and deliberate consequence of the organized insolvency of the last links of the network chain. Social exploitation follows from the orchestrated scarcity of capital of these undertakings, which leads to the employer's incapacity to pay proper wages and to comply with social obligations. The dubious financial basis of the undertakings concerned plunges the workers into a precarious situation, very much akin to social exploitation. The last criterion refers to a distinction in terms of the social exploitation's level of severity: the unbefitting conditions constitute a direct threat to the survival of the worker, they place him/her in a position of near-slavery, or they diminish the quality of his/her life in an unacceptable way. In all three cases the worker is the victim of a serious infringement of his/her right to human dignity.

Defining social exclusion is not an easy task because of the complexity and the multidimensional character of the phenomenon. The definition we propose does not have the ambition of covering exclusion in its social entirety. It refers basically to exclusion as a consequence of the functioning of the labour market. In this limited context social exclusion refers to the situation in which a person does not succeed or no longer succeeds in activating his/her labour potential on the market because of too weak a level of employability. Social exclusion may refer to a factual situation or a legal one. It concerns both the internal and external labour market. It is temporary or permanent. In legal terms social exclusion refers to a situation in which a person no longer enjoys social protection or social assistance. Even though the social State is supposed to guarantee social coverage to all citizens, reality shows that at a given moment a large number of people no longer meet the conditions to have access to the social security system. As a result, many of them are condemned to a marginal existence from which it is difficult to escape. Deprived of all social rights their exclusion becomes factual exclusion. As we have already mentioned, social exclusion can take place in the internal labour market as well as the external one. As a rule, exclusion from the internal market is covered by labour law and social security law, whereas exclusion from the external market is a matter of social security or social assistance. Depending on the duration, a distinction can be made between temporary exclusion and permanent exclusion. Both types of exclusion fall under the application of social law in the broadest possible sense.

4. FREE SOCIAL COMPETITION AND THE RIGHT TO DIGNITY AT WORK: THE NECESSITY OF SOCIAL CORRECTIONS OF THE LABOUR MARKET

4.1. FUNCTIONS AND OBJECTIVES OF SOCIAL LAW

As we have repeatedly stated, labour law and social law have a triple function. They correct the labour market and social competition, they protect workers against social exploitation and exclusion and emancipate those that are economically weak. Labour law provides the labour market with social corrections by supervising its functioning, by standardizing the pay and working conditions, and by supporting the worker in his/her development as a citizen. Social security law corrects the same labour market by organizing financial solidarity for all those who, temporarily or permanently, are excluded from the labour market for various reasons. Social law also acts protectively by trying to neutralize, correct or compensate for the economic inequality between the parties in the labour and market relations. Finally, labour law and social law support and stimulate the social emancipation of the less well-off by legitimatizing and supporting their pursuit of more economic and social equality.

4.2. CONTENT AND SCOPE OF THE CORRECTIONS

The social corrections provided for by labour law and social law do not in the least affect the legal foundations of the market economy. The freedom of work and enterprise is never questioned or threatened. On the contrary, they constitute the framework that shows the social legislators which limits cannot be crossed. As a result the capitalist production relations are not subjected to any essential modification. The labour legislators content themselves with granting the workers the right to claim participation in the decision-making within the enterprise. As for the individual relations between employers and employees, the legislators do not neutralize the economic inequality between the parties of the employment contract either, but settle for smoothing out some of the consequences, in most cases by imposing a minimum threshold of protection or by awarding monetary compensations. In short, labour law and social law are subordinate systems of market economy law. So by being directly linked to the underlying power relations the existence of social corrections is never an established fact. The adoption of fundamental social rights does not really change the situation.

4.3. CONDITIONS NECESSARY FOR THE APPLICATION OF SOCIAL CORRECTIONS

Correction of the economic relations requires the existence of an institutional framework that is favourable to readjustment of the capitalist economic order. This framework is essentially based on three elements: an adequate political structure, citizenship and a social counterforce. The nation State has been functioning as a political structure. As an expression of the will of the people, the State has the moral right to compel the economic actors to pursue a social policy. In the past the predominantly national anchoring of the market allowed the political authorities to correct the free labour market. The presence of a proper social counterforce is the second condition. The task of this complex counterforce is to influence the politicians and to convince them that it is justified to demand a social policy. The third condition refers to the existence of citizenship as a necessary instrument for the individualization of the social achievements. Citizenship makes it possible to transpose social achievements into individual rights, thus supporting the social emancipation of the workers.

4.4. LIMITS TO THE CORRECTIONS

The social corrections laid down in labour law and social law only have a limited scope. First of all they are limited because they do not question the free labour market or free social competition. Secondly, they are limited because, in essence, they only apply to wage-earners. Finally, they are limited because their scope does not go beyond national borders. The increase of the scale of the labour market as a result of the European economic integration and free global trade only underlines the weakness of the correcting system.

5. FAIR AND UNFAIR SOCIAL COMPETITION VERSUS SOCIAL DUMPING

5.1. FAIR AND UNFAIR SOCIAL COMPETITION: A LEGAL FACT

The freedom of work gives the workers the right to compete freely. When they sell their labour potential all workers decide freely (in law) on the price, the legal form and the conditions of their contract. In reality the labour market tells them what the "right" price is for their potential and this depending on their competitive position on the market. The legal form in which they wish to work determines their freedom to act. As a result self-employed workers move in a market which is less regulated than that of the wage-earners. The latter will immediately be confronted with multiple social corrections, imposed by the social rules and regulations. Even though workers have, in principle, free disposal of their labour potential and can as a result decide freely on the price for which they are prepared to sell this, in reality they are subject to the demands of those who want to employ them or make use of them as self-employed persons. As a lot of entrepreneurs themselves determine the form in which they want to hire workers, certain sectors are faced with a serious kind of social competition between wage-earners and self-employed workers, i.e. a type of competition which is certain to get harsher in those sectors where there is a lot of moonlighting or in sectors susceptible to social dumping.

As we have specified above, a distinction can be made between direct and indirect social competition, just as it is possible to make a distinction between fair and unfair social competition. The competition is direct when it takes place within the same legal or professional space. It is indirect when the competitors belong to different legal and professional spaces. By legal or professional space we mean an undertaking, a group of undertakings, a branch, a region, national territory or a segment of the labour market. Fair social competition takes places when the legal and moral rules are complied with. It becomes unfair when these rules are violated. If one respects the paradigm of the freedom of the workers in terms of law, the workers themselves are responsible for the unfair competition because they failed to make the right use of their freedom of work. Following the same reasoning, the employer and the person/company engaging self-employed workers are equally responsible if they have imposed unfair conditions.

5.2. UNFAIR SOCIAL COMPETITION AND SOCIAL DUMPING: CONGRUOUS LEGAL CONCEPTS?

In general social dumping is understood to mean practices that consist in offering the market a product or service for a price considerably lower than the average by reducing the wage costs and/or the quality of the working conditions to an extremely low level and (in most cases) contrary to the respect for human dignity. Within the European Union social dumping practices are considered to be practices that allow the social costs of a product or service to be considerably reduced by means of legal constructions that make it possible to subject workers to a national labour law arrangement other than that of the State in which the workers usually implement their employment contract. The concept of social dumping implies an element of relativity and comparison. To which entity should one refer to judge whether or not a practice can be qualified as social dumping? Is it the European labour market or the national labour market and its labour law? If the European (labour) market is taken as a reference, the right to freely choose a system of national labour law depending on the wage costs used in that system is as such not illegal. Indeed, in the European market, governed by the law of the four freedoms, no social corrections have been provided for at Union level. To answer the question with regard to the choice of a reference framework, we think the division of the powers of the European and national legislators should be taken as a basis. Except for the matters that have explicitly been granted to them, the European legislators have no competence whatsoever to legislate in matters of labour law or social law. It goes without saying that the measures in the field of market law taken on the level of the Union are not without consequences for the Member States' national legislative space regarding labour law. As a result, it is quite conceivable that by means of the market freedoms and in the absence of an adequate European labour legislation the national labour law systems are made to compete, thus entailing commercialization of those systems. That in time this process will lead to a levelling to the lowest degree of employment protection does not seem to be contrary to a legally correct interpretation of the present norms. This is not true for legal constructions which lead to social dumping by having national and foreign workers compete on the same national territory, where the latter are covered by considerably less consistent schemes of employment protection and social protection. An interpretation of the distribution of the competences that would accept situations of that kind would deprive the national legislators' competence to legislate in matters of labour law of its content. It would be an interpretation opposing the will of the parties of the Union Treaty, which does not question the sovereignty of the national labour law authors/social legislators. Therefore we think it would be advisable to take the national labour market and its national labour legislation as points of reference to decide whether certain practices are to be considered as social dumping. What is more, it is at this level that we must address the problem of the European legislators' respect for the primary fundamental right to human dignity. Indeed, in our view, the European legislators, just like their national colleagues, are obliged to safeguard human dignity in their legislative initiatives and this independently of the matter they want to regulate. Moreover, the duty to safeguard human dignity also concerns the European and national courts when they judge a case.

There can be no doubt that social dumping is an extreme form of unfair social competition. The dumping is not only a violation of the fairness in terms of social competition, it is also and foremost in contradiction to the workers' right to human dignity. Social dumping is a gross violation of this fundamental right, both relatively and absolutely. The legislative institutions have the duty to purify their legislations of provisions that give free reign to social dumping practices. The courts have to punish these practices as violations of the respect for human dignity at work.

6. SOCIAL DUMPING AND THE RIGHT TO DIGNITY AT WORK

6.1. THE RIGHT TO DIGNITY AT WORK: A PRIMARY FUNDAMENTAL RIGHT

The right to lead a life in accordance with human dignity is undoubtedly the most fundamental right of all fundamental rights. The realization of the right to human dignity presupposes respect for all the other (social) fundamental rights. In other words, respect for human dignity is the result of the application of all the other human rights.

6.2. THE ABSOLUTE AND RELATIVE SCOPE OF THE RIGHT TO HUMAN DIGNITY

As far as labour relations are concerned, the fundamental right of respect for human dignity has a relative and an absolute scope. Indeed, certain working conditions can damage human dignity depending on the context and space where they occur. Therefore, it is quite possible to qualify certain pay conditions as violations of human dignity at the European level, whereas this would be not be the case globally. For certain elements of labour relations, the severity of the violation of human dignity can be measured in terms of the surrounding social and economic circumstances. Conversely, other elements do have an absolute scope. Their occurrence in labour relations is always a violation of human dignity, independent of the place where the jobs are carried out. For example, forced labour, slavery, child labour, racism and discrimination, and prohibition of trade union freedom are always violations of human dignity.

The personal scope of the duty to respect human dignity also has an absolute and universal aspect. This duty applies to all persons or citizens, all legal persons, all political institutions. Everyone has to obey this duty, no matter the nature of the legal act or the exercised right. So all rights have to be exercised in accordance with human dignity, independently of their nature. This means all rights: civil rights, political and administrative rights, economic and financial rights, social rights, fiscal rights, penal rights, environmental rights et al. Obviously, the nature of the relations concerned determine the specific law/ right on which the obligation is based. The duty to respect human dignity is an integral part of the citizenship of all legal actors. It is a duty of care, of which the duty to respect the human dignity of others is part.

6.3. LACK OF RESPECT FOR HUMAN DIGNITY, AN INTRINSIC ELEMENT OF SOCIAL DUMPING

As we have already explained, the very concept of social dumping implies a violation of the right to respect for human dignity both in relative and/or absolute terms. Consequently, social dumping has its source in a wrong and unlawful application and interpretation of European law in the matter of freedoms of the market and competition. Thus, social dumping refers to a multiple and complex responsibility, the responsibility of the undertakings practising social dumping, the responsibility of the European judges who do not take account of or not enough account of the respect for human dignity, and most of all the responsibility of the European legislators who in their legislative initiatives systematically relegate respect for human rights to second place.

7. LACK OF RESPECT FOR HUMAN DIGNITY (AT WORK): A STRUCTURAL DEFECT OF EUROPEAN MARKET LAW?

Faithful to the neoliberal policies and the market ideology, which have inspired them from the beginning, the European legislators have made a law in which consideration for the human aspect is not a major concern. In the hierarchy of European norms the market freedoms dominate all other rights. The fundamental rights are no exception to this rule. The case law of the European courts has confirmed and reinforced the legislative options and privileged the domination of the market as a universal system of reference. This has led to the commercialization of a great deal of sections of social life. The actions of the European institutions are characterized by a constant lack of interest in fundamental rights, which has resulted in a profound contempt for the social dimension of the European citizen, a citizen who has been reduced to a pawn on the economic and financial chessboard which the European Union has become.

CHAPTER 2
HUMAN DIGNITY OF WORKERS AND COMPETITION

Wolfgang DÄUBLER*

1. POINT OF DEPARTURE: THE WORKER TREATED AS AN OBJECT

In a market economy, labour is a commodity. The economic existence of the worker depends on the development of the markets. This is obvious for self-employed workers, but employees are in a comparable situation: if the employer gets into economic difficulties, the wage earner becomes redundant and can be dismissed. As an unemployed person, he can find a new job only under the conditions determined by the market. Despite the fact that the employee is a bearer of rights vis-à-vis the employer during the employment relationship, it is misleading to call him a "citizen" of the enterprise. An individual who can be "expatriated" at any moment is no "citizen" – and the employer can always take economic decisions that make the employee redundant. In reality, the worker is treated as an object. This is in contradiction to human dignity.[1]

2. MITIGATING THE SITUATION

The fact of a person being a commodity can be more obvious or less obvious, more felt or less felt. Four factors play a role in this field.

2.1. THE INDISPENSABLE WORKER

It may happen that the worker cannot be replaced because of his special qualifications or his experience in the enterprise. To dismiss such a worker

* University of Bremen.

1 See W. DÄUBLER, *Das Grundrecht auf Mitbestimmung*, 4th edition, Frankfurt/Main 1976, pp. 129 et seq.

would create considerable problems in the working process. There is a good chance that such workers will remain in the position they desire and that their dignity is respected, especially in cases of highly qualified persons. This is a market-created protection against dismissal. Protection against dismissal is not just one element of an employee's situation: it is the fundamental condition for the exercise of all other labour law rights.[2]

2.2. PROTECTION BY LABOUR LAW

There are a lot of legal rules protecting the worker: health and safety, fundamental rights in the workplace, minimum wages, stability of real earnings, protection against dismissal. A large part consists of judge-made law, the content of which varies from country to country. These legal rules reduce the degree to which a worker is treated as a commodity. In some legal orders the employer is not allowed to examine the private life of an applicant and genetic screening is forbidden as well; the "commodity" must not be inspected in an "exaggerated" way.[3] Labour law rules are especially important for those workers who are not protected by the market. This creates considerable problems of implementation: powerful and well-equipped authorities are required in order to correct the development of the market. The gap between the law in the books and the law in action is quite a large one in most countries. The tendency towards a simple "law in the books" is especially visible in collective labour law, where the creation of institutions often depends on an initiative of the workers who elect a representative or become members of a trade union. In Germany, less than 50% of the employees in the private sector are represented by a works council; only 58% are protected by a collective agreement. The real conditions in this "shadow sector" of the economy where there is no collective labour law often escapes the notice of labour lawyers.[4]

2.3. COLLECTIVE AGREEMENTS

Even nowadays, there may be a collective counterforce defending or even increasing workers' rights. Rules in collective agreements are an important tool when it comes to the lives of workers. They improve the position of the worker

---

2 See P. Hanau, "Verfassungsrechtlicher Kündigungsschutz", in: P. Hanau, F. Heither and J. Kühling (eds.), *Richterliches Arbeitsrecht. Festschrift für Thomas Dieterich*, Munich 1999, pp. 201 et seq.

3 Cf. G. Auzero and E. Dockès, *Droit du travail*, 29th edition, Paris 2015, No 134 et seq. (French law); W. Däubler, *Gläserne Belegschaften? Das Handbuch zum Arbeitnehmerdatenschutz*, 6th edition, Frankfurt/Main 2015, No 207 et seq. (German Law).

4 Empirical evidence as to France and Germany at Artus, *Interessenhandeln jenseits der Norm*, Frankfurt/New York 2008, pp. 187 et seq.

by taking into account the concrete situation of an enterprise or a specific part of the economy like the metal industry, the textile industry or public service. In this way, they are more flexible than the law created by public authorities.[5] Unfortunately, this set of autonomous rules is now much less important in most European countries than it was 30 years ago, an obvious consequence of trade union weakness.

2.4. INFORMAL RULES

There are informal standards on "good behaviour" in many enterprises as well as in society. If they are disregarded, the workers and the public may protest. In some cases, protest of the workers will reduce productivity: for workers, the feeling of being treated in an unjust way is an obstacle to identifying themselves with their tasks and to developing valuable new ideas. Public critique, on the other hand, may damage the reputation of the enterprise. The management will be worried about losing customers – a "sanction" which can hurt the enterprise much more than a two-week strike, the consequences of which will be dealt with by overtime work within a month.[6] The existence of these informal rules, as well as the moral values and the social consciousness of the population, differ from country to country.

3. RETURNING TO THE MARKET FORCES

The four factors are of a quite precarious nature.

The mechanisms of the market do not always provide reliable protection. Although it is in the interest of an employer not to lose qualified and experienced workers, one can never exclude the possibility that some employers may damage their own interests through their actions. The protection disappears if the enterprise (or part of it) is closed for economic or other reasons. Highly qualified people will rapidly find a new job. People whose "value" depends on long experience in the plant will lose their "human capital" and will often find themselves in a comparable situation on the labour market as unqualified workers.

Neoliberalism reduces legal protection, especially in the field of employment stability, because it is considered to be an unnecessary obstacle to market freedom. Workers find themselves in a weaker position than before. Criticism of neoliberalism is considered a defence of out-dated structures. In some countries,

---

5 As to the inherent flexibility of labour law see W. Däubler, "Die Flexibilität des Arbeitsrechts", in: *Festschrift Dieterich*, above n. 2, p. 63 et seq.

6 See J.-E. Ray, *Droit Social*, 2003, p. 591: *"Economie de la réputation"*.

like Britain, deregulation is possible by a majority decision of Parliament, whereas in other countries an amendment of the constitution would be necessary.

Neoliberalism brings individualistic ideologies with it which in fact attract a lot of workers and their unions. The consequence is a reduction in union density in many countries and decreasing importance of collective agreements. Once again, workers lose a significant part of their protection.

Even informal rules will no longer function in the same way as before. Moral standards become less strict if the argument that "this is a consequence of the market" has a great deal of authority in public reasoning: if the free market is the best way of organizing the economy, one has to accept social disadvantages. Widespread criticism can be found in extreme cases only.

As a result of neoliberalism, the number of people whose dignity is in danger is increasing considerably. In some societies, the majority of workers may remain without effective protection.

4. INTERNATIONALIZATION OF THE MARKETS

Globalization is perhaps the most important economic basis for the success of the neoliberal ideology. Not only is there social competition but also what may be called social dumping. Countries with a low wage level and/or a favourable currency exchange rate can offer goods and some services at a very low price. Enterprises from industrialized countries invest in these countries and make use of the comparative advantage for their products. The first well-known example of this strategy was the textile industry during the 1970s;[7] other industries followed. In high-wage countries enterprises limit themselves to producing very sophisticated products. A new international division of labour appears.

Internationalized production is not confronted with international labour law rules. Although there are UN and ILO Conventions, they are normally not implemented in low-wage countries. Although there is a patchwork of national rules, those rules are mostly of no real importance in developing countries. Some enterprises have concluded framework agreements with international trade unions but their legal value seems doubtful. It is difficult if not impossible to control their application, and local subcontractors are usually not included in the conclusion of such agreements.[8]

---

7 Cf. F. Fröbel, J. Heinrichs and O. Kreye, *Die neue internationale Arbeitsteilung*, Reinbek 1977.

8 Cf. B. Hepple, *Labour Laws and Global Trade*, Oxford/Portland 2005; R. Zimmer, *Soziale Mindeststandards und ihre Durchsetzungsmechanismen. Sicherung internationaler Mindeststandards durch Verhaltenskodizes?*, Baden-Baden 2008.

In the EU, the freedom to deliver services implies the right of employers to send their workers to another Member State. If the average wage level "at home" is 10% of the wage level in the country where the work is done, social dumping will automatically occur. The EC Directive on Posted Workers[9] offers a modest level of protection. Some fundamental rules like health protection and minimum wages apply, but there is no further adaptation to the social standards of the host country. In the construction sector collective agreements about minimum wages and annual leave apply; the Member States can include other parts of the economy too. The directive is interpreted by the European Court of Justice in such a way that other rules in collective agreements (e.g. about normal wages) do not apply. The Court considers the directive to be exhaustive, defining at the same time the highest possible wage level.[10] It is quite difficult to check whether minimum standards are observed in concrete cases since national authorities are not allowed to have a look at the workers' bank accounts in their home countries. Contributions to the social security system are often quite low, because they are calculated on the basis of minimum wages and require a lower percentage than in the host country. The comparative cost advantage remains quite important. Labour standards in the host countries are therefore under pressure. This brings a short-term advantage to the less developed Member States, which they consider to be essential. But even from a medium-term perspective, it will prove to be a disadvantage: instead of developing the productivity of their own economies, the countries of origin earn money by sending their most flexible workers abroad. No transfer of technology occurs. Although this was already a topic of discussion in the 1970s,[11] societies do not always learn from the past.

5. USING INFORMATION TECHNOLOGY

Information technology, especially the Internet, facilitates the recourse to low-price services in developing countries. Growing importance is attached to so-called crowdworking:[12] an enterprise in Europe or the US offers small tasks on the Internet which can be performed by workers all over the world. The prices are quite low because there are a lot of competitors from low-wage countries. Estimates show that in many cases the income amounts to approximately

9 Directive 96/71/EC of the European Parliament and of the Council of 16 December 1996 concerning the posting of workers in the framework of the provision of services, *OJ L* 181997, 1–6.

10 ECJ 11 December 2007, Case C-438/05, *Viking*; ECJ 18 December 2007, Case C-341/05, *Laval*.

11 See W. Däubler, "Zur rechtlichen und sozialen Situation der Gastarbeiter in der BRD", *Demokratie und Recht* (DuR) 1974, pp. 3–35.

12 Cf. the contributions in: C. Benner (ed.), *Crowdwork – zurück in die Zukunft? Perspektiven digitaler Arbeit*, Frankfurt/Main 2014.

US $2/hour.[13] For more complicated tasks, there are two kinds of contracts. The first one is (relatively) fair: interested people can declare their willingness to do the "job" and mention the conditions; the best offer will be accepted. The second one is not so fair: everyone who is interested is invited to perform the task but only the best person will earn money; the others have worked for nothing and have even had to transfer all their copyrights to the enterprise.[14] Recently, there was a lawsuit in California dealing with the question whether the practice of crowdworking contradicts the Minimum Wage Act of California and the US Fair Labor Standards Act.[15] Crowdworkers only stand a chance of invoking labour law rules if the notion of "employee" is interpreted broadly.[16] In this particular case, a settlement was reached which resulted in 65% of the money going to the lawyers and only a modest pay increase for the crowdworkers.[17]

6. PROPOSALS TO IMPROVE THE SITUATION

6.1. BETTER TRADE UNIONS?

The decrease in union membership is not a universal trend. There are some exceptions like Sweden and Belgium which could serve as examples to other countries.[18] Why not use the "best practice" in this field? The obvious objection is that trade unions are embedded in a national tradition of industrial relations which cannot be transferred to other countries. If in one country the trade unions manage unemployment insurance – which can be quite important when it comes to attracting new members – there is no realistic chance of implementing this model in a country where trade unions have already lost a great deal of their influence.

Traditional trade unions often resemble an industrial plant with its hierarchic setting: there is a CEO and a board of directors at the top, there are department leaders and group leaders, and there are normal collaborators. Just like in big enterprises, new ideas are not easily accepted: will they not create a lot of work?

---

13 J.M. Leimeister and S. Zogaj, *Neue Arbeitsorganisation durch Crowdsourcing*, Hans-Böckler-Stiftung, Düsseldorf 2013, available at: www.boeckler.de/pdf/p_arbp_287.pdf.

14 The question whether this is compatible with the German Civil Code is examined by W. Däubler, "Crowdworker – Schutz auch außerhalb des Arbeitsrechts?", in: C. Benner (ed.), above n. 12, pp. 243, 253 et seq.

15 *Otey, et al., v. Crowdflower*, United States District Court Northern District of California, Case No 12-cv-05524-JST.

16 For US law see M.A. Cherry, "Working for (Virtually) Minimum Wage: Applying the Fair Labor Standards Act in Cyberspace", *Alabama Law Review* 60, 2009, p. 1077 et seq.

17 Www.staffingindustry.com/Research-Publications/Daily-News.

18 Overview of membership in different European countries established by the European Trade Union Institute (ETUI): http://de.worker-participation.eu/Nationale-Arbeitsbeziehungen/Quer-durch-Europa/Gewerkschaften.

Will they perhaps have an adverse effect? Are they really compatible with the principles laid down in the general programme? Could their realization change the balance between different departments? There are so many questions with no clear answers. Would it not be reasonable to renounce such a hazardous game? This description refers to a couple of German experiences which hopefully cannot be generalized. Nevertheless, sociologists agree that the traditional structure is not adequate if you are looking for experience and innovation. Enterprises have changed a lot for the same reason too.

In the US, there is a "National Day Laborer Organizing Network" with member organizations across the different states. The main centre of the network is located in California.[19] Some points seem to be of general interest. Day workers are organized into a "network". There are so-called contact persons covering different areas of larger towns. They inform members of the normal rate for a certain activity and which employers are good and which are bad. Bad employers will, of course, be avoided. If many people consult the contact person, bad employers will have difficulties finding day workers at all. The union gives information that can lead to a kind of boycott. We can find the same principle in the movement of the "travelling journeymen" (*Gesellenbewegung* in German) which came into existence in Central Europe in the 13th century. Bad employers, i.e. (at that time) craftsmen, were formally "discredited"; no journeyman could conclude a contract with them without also being discredited himself.[20] In a way, boycotts replace strikes and other forms of collective actions.

Can this form of organization gain prominence in modern Europe? There are some advantages of a network in comparison with traditional labour movement organizations.

The people involved have a clear objective and a well-defined role. The information given to a member (or even to other persons) is obviously useful and can therefore justify a small monthly fee.

Repressing a network is difficult. Meetings between two or three people cannot be controlled by the authorities, and the contact can easily be declared to be of a private nature.

Ideological differences play no role. The fulfilment of the organization's function does not depend on the political opinions of the people involved. The collaboration merely requires the conviction that the situation of day workers should be improved. It is not relevant whether this conviction comes from a Christian, socialist or communist point of view.

New ideas developed by a contact person may be realized at once. Each collaborator can try to carry out his tasks in a better way – there is no hierarchy and therefore no person with more authority who needs to give his approval.

---

19 Http://ndlon.org.

20 See W. Däubler, in: W. Däubler (ed.), *Arbeitskampfrecht*, 3rd edition, Baden-Baden 2011, §1 Rn 5 et seq. (with further references).

Is such a network not the only solution when it comes to organizing crowdworkers?

The network solution is, however, not universally appropriate. The issue with a network is that there is a certain level of instability – the value of the information may be doubtful. If that is indeed the case, people will seek information elsewhere. However, there is one fact which is difficult to ignore. Many lawyers who are on the side of workers are part of such networks: one or several law firms of this kind can be found in larger towns and they are usually in contact with comparable law firms in other towns. There are even networks all over Europe. It would be very difficult to bring these people together in the same political party, but collaboration in the interest of workers is possible. It is even possible to find people who have maintained the same political position as they had in the 1970s and 1980s, whereas trade unions have often given it up without replacing it with a new standpoint.

6.2. MOBILIZING PUBLIC OPINION

Schlecker, a German retail chain, has had a very specific reputation for years. For a long time, they had trouble with their works councils, whose rights were often neglected. The press wrote about it and the majority of newspapers supported the works councils as the underdogs. Eventually, Schlecker fully recognized the legal situation and the discussion calmed down. However, the story continued. Schlecker had economic difficulties and restructured a large number of shops. A lot of small shops were merged into a single bigger one. Workers were dismissed. During the period of notice, they received a "kind offer" to come to a firm called Meniar, which was an abbreviation for "bringing people into jobs" (*Menschen in Arbeit*). Meniar was a temporary employment agency and a wholly owned branch of Schlecker. Workers were offered new contracts with wages more than 35% below their former level. Those who accepted were sent to a shop quite near the place where they had worked before; sometimes it was even the same shop. They had to perform the same kind of work as before, but for much lower wages.

Trade unions protested but were not able to organize a strike. The media gave critical reports. The majority of the population was on the side of the workers and some lawyers tried to prove that the way these workers were being treated was a circumvention of the law guaranteeing acquired rights in cases of transfer of enterprises and plants. However, this was not decisive for the company. In the end, the volume of sales went down and it seemed likely that this was a consequence of the public campaign. The owners decided to close down Meniar, their temporary employment agency, thus improving their reputation and winning back their customers.[21] Workers also had their previous salaries restored.

21 www.zeit.de/wirtschaft/2010-01/schlecker-meniar-kuendigung.

This story illustrates some features which are never dealt with in labour law. Let us assume a union density of 80% in the shops of Schlecker. The union would decide to fight against the intended reduction in wages, demanding that Meniar goes out of business. Of course, Schlecker would refuse and the union would threaten the firm with a strike. What would be the consequence? Schlecker would take this to the labour tribunal to get an injunction against the trade union. The strike would be prohibited because of its illegal aim: to continue or not to continue a business is a so-called entrepreneurial decision which must not be an object of a collective agreement or a strike.[22] One could organize a strike for better working conditions at Meniar – but even then it is doubtful whether workers not affected by the measures would be able to participate in a kind of solidarity strike. All these legal obstacles do not exist if the press advocate the end of the temporary employment agency and if a number of consumers go to another firm. It becomes an advantage for the workers to leave the sphere of collective bargaining. Dear labour law colleagues – please bear this in mind!

What is possible in Germany may happen in China, too. On 1 January 2008, the new labour contract law came into force. One of its provisions contained the rule that after ten years of service with the same employer a fixed-term contract is automatically transformed into an open-ended contract. Huawei, an IT firm, had a lot of employees who fulfilled this condition. The enterprise "asked" them to cancel the employment contract in October or November 2007. In the beginning of January they would receive a new fixed-term contract with the conditions they had before. Legally it was as doubtful as Schlecker's strategy, but it is difficult for a worker who wants to continue his employment to go to court. However, the press intervened: it seemed to be obvious that the new rule was being circumvented. Huawei gave in and granted open-ended contracts to all workers concerned.[23]

As in the Schlecker case, it would have been risky to use the route of labour law. It was quite unclear how the courts would have decided: if it was obvious that Huawei pressed workers to sign a cancellation contract, the court would probably have decided in favour of the workers. But what would have happened if the pressure could not be proven? The employer would merely have argued that the worker asked for unpaid leave. Why not? There is no need to use the suspension of the employment contract; an interruption of the contractual relationship is also admissible.

How is public opinion able to get such results? The first requirement is the personal commitment of some critical journalists and a political framework that allows such reports. Usually, a private owner of a newspaper will not oppose such

22 That is at least the prevailing opinion in Gemany; see W. Däubler, above n. 20, §13 Note 36 et seq.

23 www.wiwo.de/unternehmen/huawei-umstrittener-chinesischer-export-seite-3/5469512-3.html.

articles as long as the articles in question will be read and the newspaper will be quoted. The second requirement is that a lot of people share the social value that over-exploitation is unacceptable and immoral. That is still the case in Germany as well as in France or Spain; it is less likely, however, that this will be the case in the United States as well. In China, capitalist exploitation is still considered a transitional phenomenon; the large majority of people will accept criticism of excesses. Sharing certain values is a much lower threshold than engaging in trade union activities or a strike. Even the boycotting of certain goods does not require a lot of courage. Public pressure can therefore be organized much more easily than traditional collective actions.

Most enterprises are quite sensitive as to their public reputation – another advantage for the workers. They never know if a newspaper article will have a negative impact on their turnover. The risk of losing customers seems to be much more important than the reduction of wage costs (the latter of which is usually the reason for socially unacceptable measures). This sensitivity is very high in the case of retail firms that have direct contact with the consumers, but it is less developed with heavy industry which sells its products to the State (e.g. weapons) or exclusively to other enterprises.

However, criticism of the behaviour of undertakings does not always deal with clear facts like in the Schlecker or Huawei cases. It may happen that the enterprise denies the accusation, affirming that everything is fine. The company may go to court to get an injunction giving it the right to publish a counter-statement. If the information comes from an employee, he faces the problems of being a whistleblower, whose position is quite ambiguous, poised between traitor and hero. The European Court of Human Rights has strengthened the position of such people by enabling them to invoke the freedom of opinion even in cases in which the facts cannot be proven. This fundamental right is restricted only if the facts are wrong and the whistleblower has acted with gross negligence.[24]

What is true for the press and television is also true for the Internet. Whether a blog can replace a newspaper in a certain way and become a starting point of a campaign depends on the actual role of the Internet in the country in question. In the near future, it will be a decisive forum in terms of influencing public opinion everywhere. The Internet differs from the press and television, however, in the fact that it has a more democratic character: one no longer needs critical "journalists"; a few critical bloggers can fulfil the same function. On Twitter and other social media, popular people can have many "followers" who automatically receive all their statements. The Chilean student leader Camila Vallejo, for instance, has 874,000 followers,[25] which is equivalent to the power of a large newspaper. In a way, the Internet offers more possibilities to individuals than

---

24 European Court of Human Rights 21 July 2011, Appl. No 28274/08, *Heinisch*, NZA 2011, 1269.

25 https://twitter.com/camila_vallejo.

other media have ever done before. If a few people give a good and convincing evaluation of an event, that can be the starting point for a campaign against socially unacceptable behaviour of enterprises and managers.

6.3. COLLECTIVE ACTION ON THE INTERNET

More and more work is done via the Internet. One can use it to support collective actions in the "real world" and one can disturb the working process via the Internet.

As to the first alternative, I would like to mention the collective actions realized by workers and their friends against IBM Italy. Like in other countries, there is the Internet platform "Second Life". Anyone can create a virtual human being (avatar) with certain good and certain bad qualities. In 2007, about 3,000 people from more than 30 countries "played" the collective bargaining process at IBM Italy, adding some important modifications to the reality: hundreds of pickets were present, large demonstrations took place and a meeting of the board of directors could not continue because many strikers entered the room. The decision-makers were highly impressed; would it not be possible for the actions in the game to become reality? The next day an agreement was signed in which IBM renounced all intended wage reductions.[26] This situation is similar to a public campaign: unlike in a strike, the individuals did not run any risk. For some of them, participation may even have been a fun activity providing a nice change to the routine of everyday life.

IT technology can also be disrupted. In 2002, there was a new form of collective action against the German company Lufthansa. The company had collaborated with the government to return to their home countries people who had tried to obtain political asylum in Germany but were not successful. It was clear that many of them would go to prison on arrival in their country of origin; some of them would even be tortured or put to death. A group of citizens protested against this. They developed the following slogan: "Three classes with Lufthansa – economy class, business class, deportation class". The conflict escalated when a Nigerian citizen arrived dead in his country despite being accompanied by two German policemen. The group decided to block the Lufthansa booking system by sending so many e-mails that it would break down. They developed new software which sent three e-mails to the Lufthansa computer every second. The Lufthansa website was offline for a couple of hours but the company then found a way around this problem by using other

26 Cf. P. Berg, E. Kocher, H. Platow, C. Schoof and D. Schumann, *Tarifvertrags- und Arbeitskampfrecht, Kompaktkommentar*, 4th edition, Frankfurt/Main 2013, AKR Rn. 224.

computers. One of the members of the group was prosecuted for duress but was acquitted by the Frankfurt Court of Appeal.[27]

Other forms of protest are considered to be illegal sabotage. In one case, a computer scientist had been dismissed and was about to be replaced by a private firm. He installed a very sophisticated computer virus which blocked the whole system two days after he left his job. The new firm was quite helpless. As a second firm could not find the reason either, he was asked to come back as a "subcontractor" for a short time in order to repair the system. After some hours he succeeded in repairing the system but he installed a new virus which became effective two weeks later. So once again, he was asked to come back until his method was accidentally discovered.[28] In another case, a computer scientist changed the main passwords of his employer before leaving so the firm was paralysed for several days.[29] Another story concerns a system administrator: he modified programmes in such a way that everything was deleted if the words "dismissed by the employer" appeared in his personal file.

7. PERSPECTIVES

The decline of trade unions and collective bargaining is not the end of defending workers' interests. Labour lawyers will perhaps be forced to look into other fields of law such as freedom of the press, consumers' activities and Internet communication. In the medium and long term this mode of action could even be more efficient than traditional collective bargaining. In that case, it may be good to advise employers: defend collective bargaining! You will be better off! This can (and should) be an object of further discussion.

---

27 OLG Frankfurt/Main 22 May 2006, 1 Sa 319/05, CR (Computer und Recht) 2006, 684.

28 See LAG (Landesarbeitsgericht) Saarland 1 December 1993, 3 Sa 154/92, Beilage 7/1994 zu BB S. 14.

29 See LAG Hessisch 13 May 2002, 13 Sa 1268/01, RDV (Recht der Datenverarbeitung) 2003, 148.

CHAPTER 3

SOCIAL DUMPING: A SYMPTOM OF THE EUROPEAN CONSTRUCTION

An Exploratory Study of Social Dumping in Road Transport

Jan BUELENS* and Lies MICHIELSEN**

1. INTRODUCTION

In this contribution we will discuss how the European construction leads to social dumping practices. Even though the focus is on the road transport sector, our analysis and some of our proposals also apply to other sectors.[1]

Because of its very nature the transport sector is one of the key industries of the European internal market and a textbook example for the analysis of the functioning of the European Union.

Since the beginning of the liberalization process in the 1990s and the ensuing ever-growing competition, the road freight transport sector has undergone several major changes. Thanks to EU regulations, cross-border transport enterprises came into existence. By establishing a company in Eastern Europe, it is easy for road transport operators to use East European lorries and drivers in Belgium, not only to organize international transport but also for domestic transport activities.[2] As a result of the introduction of cabotage rights on 1 July 1998, all businesses within the EU can offer transport services in a host Member State. These changes became even more prominent after the enlargement of the EU in three steps, i.e. in 2004, 2007 and 2013, with thirteen new Member States.

* Professor of Labour Law, University of Antwerp.

** Lawyer with Progress Lawyers Network.

1 The scientific research, financed by the European Social Fund and the Flemish Government, was carried out by Jan Buelens and Lies Michielsen (lies.michielsen@progresslaw.net) under the supervision of Professor M. Rigaux.

2 Although cabotage transport is subject to conditions it is not easy to monitor this.

The policy and the legislation of the European Union were and are almost completely imbued with the further development of the liberalization process. No equivalent attention has been paid to social rights or upward social harmonization in the field of employment and working conditions.[3]

The differences in terms of labour and social market structures in the EU countries are huge. The launch of an internal market and a common transport policy, together with the extension of the EU to the south and the east, in combination with weak enforcement, is the ideal breeding ground for social dumping practices. These practices raise serious questions with regard to the content and effectiveness of the European legislative and enforcement schemes and have consequences for the social rights of both resident and non-resident professional drivers.[4] Moreover, there is the danger that as a result of "social policy regime competition" between Member States, national governments will be put under pressure to lower their employment and social standards in order to cut the high wage costs for companies.

The findings of the study on Social and Working Conditions of Road Transport Hauliers of the Directorate General Internal Policies of the European Parliament of 2013 show that the working environment (including a higher level of discrimination between EU15[5] and EU12 drivers), job demands (i.e. a higher degree of task flexibility and more non-driving activities) and income levels (i.e. a continuous drop in drivers' salary levels) are the social components that have deteriorated the most over the past five years.[6] In concrete terms the competition in working conditions and circumstances resulted over a period of five years (2008–2013) in, among other things, an average of 30–40% loss of income of drivers in the Union as a whole, an increase of working hours and a deterioration of the working conditions.[7]

True, there are European rules and regulations on some aspects of working conditions (driving time and rest periods, etc.), but the question is whether this is enough.

In the first section we will analyse the structure of the European Union, the position granted to the fundamental social rights and the relationship between

---

3 S. Giubboni, "Social Rights and Market Freedom in the European Constitution: A Re-Appraisal", *European Labour Law Journal*, Volume 1 (2010), No 2, 162–163; F.W. Scharpf, "The European Social Model: Coping with the Challenges of Diversity", *Journal of Common Market Studies*, Volume 6 (2002), 45; H. Verschueren, "Cross-border Workers in the European Internal Market", *International Journal of Comparative Labour Law and Industrial Relations*, Volume 2 (2008), 167–168.

4 Non-resident drivers are drivers who work from a country other than their own.

5 With the entry of Croatia this has now become EU16.

6 Study on Social and Working Conditions of Road Transport Hauliers of the Directorate General Internal Policies of the European Parliament, Policy Department B: Structural and Cohesion Policies, Transport and Tourism, 2013, available at: www.europarl.europa.eu/RegData/etudes/etudes/join/2013/495855/IPOL-TRAN_ET(2013)495855_EN.pdf.

7 Directorate General for Internal Policies – Social and working conditions of road transport hauliers, 2013, p. 20.

these fundamental rights and the economic freedoms. In the second section we will map out the European rules and regulations relevant to the road transport sector. We will conclude with a number of avenues to combat social dumping in road transport.

Before mapping out the relevant European legislation we want to explain one of the key concepts in this chapter, i.e. "social dumping".

There is no universally accepted definition of social dumping but several scholars have tried to define the concept.[8]

According to the European Trade Union Institute (ETUI), social dumping can be defined as follows:

> "a conscious strategy involving the lowering of wage and employment standards, driven by companies seeking to gain a competitive advantage over other market participants, and indirectly involving their workers as well as home and host country governments"[9]

and:

> "the practice undertaken by self-interested market participants, of undermining or evading existing social regulations with the aim of gaining a competitive advantage".[10]

In this contribution we understand "social dumping" to mean: the use of professional drivers from countries with a lower level of pay and working conditions and employment protection in countries with a higher level.

---

8 Some examples: J. Alber and G. Standing, "Social dumping, catch-up or convergence? Europe in a comparative global context", *Journal of European Social Policy*, Volume 10 (1990), No 2, 99–119; D. Vaughan-Whitehead, *EU Enlargement versus Social Europe? The uncertain future of the European Social Model*, Edward Elgar, Cheltenham 2003; H.-W. Sinn, "Social dumping in the transformation process?", NBER Working Paper 8364, Cambridge, MA, National Bureau of Economic Research; H. Mosley, "The 'social dumping' threat of European integration: a critique", in: B. Unger and F. Van Waarden (eds.), *Convergence or diversity? Internationalization and economic policy response*, Avebury, Aldershot 1995, pp. 182–199; P. Pochet, "Dumping social: un concept operationnel?", *Nota Bene* (1990), 56, 1–4.

9 M. Bernaciak, "Social dumping: political catchphrase or threat to labour standards?", Brussels, ETUI Working Paper, 2012, p. 32, Collection 2012. On the same issue, see the definitions respectively provided by the European Conference of Ministers of Transport (ECMT) and the European Foundation for the Improvement of Living and Working Conditions (Eurofound). The ECMT defines social dumping practices as "the deliberate infringement, circumvention or erosion of applicable social legislation in force – at either the national, Community or international level – in order to procure an advantage, notably a competitive advantage" (ECMT, 2002). Eurofound describes social dumping as "a practice involving the export of goods from a country with weak or poorly enforced labour standards, where the exporter costs are artificially lower than its competitors in countries with higher standards, hence representing an unfair advantage in international trade" (Eurofound, 2012).

10 M. Bernaciak, "Social dumping and the EU integration process", ETUI Working Paper, 2014.

A term which is frequently used as a synonym for social dumping is "unfair competition". We define unfair competition as an unfair, unethical and often illegal attempt to achieve a competitive advantage by means of false, unethical or fraudulent trade practices. Social dumping is a form of unfair competition.

2. THE EUROPEAN CONSTRUCTION

In this chapter we analyse the European structure, one of the main causes of social dumping.

In the first section of this chapter we will go through the principles of the Treaty on the Functioning of the European Union (TFEU) (section 2.1). First, we will discuss the separate title given to transport in the TFEU as a key factor of the European economy (section 2.1.1). Second, the free movement of workers, the freedom of establishment and the free movement of services will be dealt with (section 2.1.2). The latter two in particular are the driving forces behind social dumping. Subsequently, we will analyse the case law which has been decisive for the interpretation of free movement. We conclude with the restrictions on free movement as laid down in law and developed in case law.

In the second section the Charter on Fundamental Rights of the European Union is discussed (section 2.2). We will conclude with the relationship between these fundamental rights and the economic freedoms (section 2.3).

2.1. TREATY ON THE FUNCTIONING OF THE EUROPEAN UNION

2.1.1. Separate title on transport in the TFEU: a common transport policy

The establishment of a common transport market was one of the first policies of the European Community.

The EU's competence to liberalize the transport sector does not result from the general chapter on free movement of services of Article 56 et seq. of the TFEU, but instead from the separate title "Transport" (Article 90 et seq. of the TFEU).

The liberalization of transport policies was already planned at the time of the establishment of the European Economic Community in 1957. For this purpose the EC Treaty instructed the Council of Ministers to lay down, before the end of the transition period and at the latest by the end of 1969, common rules for international transport and to determine the conditions under which transport operators are allowed to provide cabotage services in a Member State.[11]

11 Article 75 of the EEC Treaty; A.T.J.M. Jacobs and E.J.M. Van Herk, "Sociale aspecten van de Europese liberalisering van het beroepsgoederenvervoer over de weg", *SEW* 3, 1995, March, 155–158.

As a consequence of conflicts of interests between the Member States and their fear of a competitive struggle, hardly any progress was made in the liberalization of road haulage in the European Union in the following years. In 1983, fed up as it was with the delays, the European Parliament took the case to the European Court of Justice claiming that the Council had failed to establish a common transport policy.[12] The Court confirmed that the Council had breached the treaty and ordered the Council to take the required measures within "a reasonable period". Together with the White Paper of the European Commission on the completion of the internal market[13] this judgment stimulated the decision-making process. Since 1 January 1993 a transport operator established in an EU Member State can freely carry out road transport activities to another Member State with a Community transport authorization.[14] Before that time a special licence was required. All operators could now carry out international transport operations provided they fulfil the qualitative criteria as described in Directive 74/561 on the access to the occupation of road haulage operator in national and international transport operations.[15] The Commission can intervene if there is a risk of the market being disturbed.[16]

The common transport policy was developed in order to remove obstacles at the borders between the Member States with a view to contributing to the free movement of persons and goods. The main objective of this policy is the completion of the internal transport market.

As far as international road transport is concerned, the liberalization has now been completed. As regards cabotage this is not yet the case (see 3.3).

For the sake of completeness we also mention that on 1 December 1992 the Benelux countries opened their national road transport for transport operators from the other Member States of the Benelux.[17]

---

12 Pursuant to Article 175 EEC Treaty; Case C-13/83, *European Parliament v. the Council of the EC*, 22 May 1985, 1513, *SEW*, 1985, 786, with comment by H.G. Schermers and P.J. Slot.

13 European Commission, "Completing the Internal Market", Brussels, 14 June 1985, COM (85) 310 fin.

14 Article 3 Council Regulation (EEC) No 881/92 of 26 March 1992 on access to the market in the carriage of goods by road within the Community to or from the territory of a Member State or passing across the territory of one or more Member States, *OJ L* 1992/95, 1 amended by Regulation (EC) No 484/2002, *OJ L* 2002/76.

15 Directive 74/561 on admission to the occupation of road haulage operator in national and international transport operations, *OJ L* 1974/308, 18.

16 Council Regulation (EEC) No 3916/90 of 21 December 1990 on measures to be taken in the event of a crisis in the market in the carriage of goods by road, *OJ L* 1990/375, 10, and Council Regulation (EEC) No 881/92 of 26 March 1992 on access to the market in the carriage of goods by road within the Community to or from the territory of a Member State or passing across the territory of one or more Member States, *OJ L* 1992/95, 1 amended by Regulation (EC) No 484/2002, *OJ L* 2002/76.

17 Compare Decision of the Committee of Ministers of the Benelux of 16 December 1991 on the establishment of the conditions under which undertakings established in a Benelux country are allowed access to road transport, M (91) 20.

2.1.2. *Free movement of workers, freedom of establishment and free movement of services*

Of the various freedoms the freedom of establishment is the most essential for the road transport sector. However, since the prohibition of discrimination applying to the free movement of workers and the case law of the Court of Justice on the free movement of services also play an important role in the social dumping issue, this free movement of workers and services will also be discussed.

2.1.2.1. Free movement of workers

One of the four freedoms of the EU is the free movement of persons[18] which means that a person, a citizen of the European Union,[19] must be able to move freely within the European Union.

This freedom of movement for persons as laid down in Article 45 TFEU (former Article 39 EC Treaty)[20] relates in the first place to workers. Those who want to work in another Member State must be able to do so without restrictions. As regards employment, remuneration and other working conditions, Article 45 TFEU prohibits discrimination on grounds of nationality. A worker from another Member State must be treated on the labour market as a Member State's own national.[21]

The present EU's legal provisions on the free movement of workers can be found in Regulation 1612/68[22] and in Residence Directive 2004/38.[23]

---

18 In addition to the free movement of services (Articles 49–55 EC Treaty), goods (Articles 23–31 EC Treaty) and capital (Articles 56–60 EC Treaty). However, these last two freedoms are not relevant for the research.

19 The provisions also apply to the European Economic Area (EEA). These are the EU Member States plus Norway, Iceland, Liechtenstein and, since 1 June 2004, Switzerland.

20 Treaty establishing the European Community of 25 March 1957, *Trb.* 1957, 74 and 91, for a consolidated version of the EC Treaty, see *OJ C* 2002/325, 1.

21 H. Verschueren, *Grensoverschrijdende arbeid,* Die Keure, Bruges 2000, p. 123.

22 Regulation (EEC) No 1612/68 of the Council of 15 October 1968 on free movement of workers within the Community, *OJ L* 1968/257. Meanwhile this regulation has been replaced by Regulation (EU) No 492/2011 of the European Parliament and of the Council of 5 April 2011 on freedom of movement for workers within the Union, *OJ L* 2011/141, 1. As far as content is concerned this new regulation hardly introduced any changes in the provisions of the old regulation.

23 Correcting Directive 2004/38/EC of the European Parliament and of the Council of 29 April 2004 on the right of citizens of the Union and their family members to move and reside freely within the territory of the Member States amending Regulation (EEC) No 1612/68 and repealing Directives 64/221/EEC, 68/360/EEC, 72/194/EEC, 73/148/EEC, 75/34/EEC, 75/35/EEC, 90/364/EEC, 90/365/EEC and 93/96/EEC, *OJ L* 2004/229, 35.

In the regulation the general prohibition of discrimination has been developed further.[24] It lays down that as far as the conditions for accepting and performing work are concerned no distinction may be made between a Member State's own citizens and citizens of other Member States.[25] If employment of foreign workers is restricted by quota systems (per undertaking, sector, region or at a national level), these quotas may not be applied to nationals of other Member States.[26] The right to equal treatment in terms of working conditions is also repeated in the regulation.[27] Moreover, Article 8 refers explicitly to collective rights, stating that migrant workers also have the same right to join trade unions.

2.1.2.2. Freedom of establishment

Self-employed persons, practitioners of the professions and legal persons within the meaning of Article 54 TFEU who are legitimately active in a Member State may carry out economic activities in another Member State in a permanent manner (freedom of establishment: Article 49 TFEU) or temporarily offer and provide services in other Member States while remaining in their country of origin (freedom to provide services: Article 56 TFEU).

The freedom of establishment includes the right to access to activities other than work for wages and the exercise thereof, as well as the establishment and management of undertakings for the purpose of permanent activities, under the same conditions as the Member State of establishment has regulated by law for its own nationals.

2.1.2.3. Free movement of services

The freedom to provide services applies to all services which are, as a rule, carried out for remuneration, in so far as the provisions on the free movement of goods, capital and persons do not apply. For this purpose the person providing a service can temporarily pursue his/her activities in the Member State where the service is offered under the same conditions as those established by the Member State for its own nationals.

Article 57(1) TFEU defines services as "services normally provided for remuneration, in so far as they are not governed by the provisions relating to

---

24 Devos refers to a chronological cascade of rights, going from the right to leave the country of origin to derived rights after the termination of the employment relationship, see K. Devos, *Detachering binnen de Europese Unie: La revanche del tango de Europa*, UGA, Kortrijk 2006, p. 31.

25 Article 3 (1) Regulation 1612/68.

26 Article 4(1) Regulation 1612/68. The second paragraph of this article stipulates that when the granting of certain benefits is subject to a minimum percentage of national workers being employed, nationals of other Member States shall be counted as national workers.

27 Article 7(1) Regulation 1612/68; moreover, Article 7(4) Regulation 1612/68 states that any discriminatory clause of collective or individual agreements shall be null and void.

freedom of goods, capital and persons". According to Article 56 TFEU all restrictions on the freedom to provide services within the Community are forbidden.

The free movement of services in the field of transport is regulated by the provisions in the title on transport.[28]

2.1.2.4. The case law of the Court of Justice

The case law of the Court of Justice has been decisive for the interpretation of the freedom of establishment and the freedom to provide services as we know it.

The European Court of Justice has tested legislation aimed at imposing working conditions and circumstances going beyond the mandatory provisions for minimum protection of temporarily employed workers in that Member State against the right to free movement. In addition, the Court has ruled on the interaction between the use of collective bargaining and the right to strike and the free movement of services.

For instance in 1990 in *Rush Portuguesa*[29] the Court ruled that Articles 49 and 50 (former Articles 59 and 60) EC Treaty do not allow a Member State to prohibit service providers established in another Member State from moving freely with their employees on its territory. The movement of the employees in question may not be subjected to restrictive conditions either[30] unless they are temporary agency workers.[31]

In *Vander Elst* the Court ruled that a service provider established in another Member State can indeed make use of his/her employees lawfully residing in that Member State even if these workers are nationals of countries not belonging to the European Union, at least if after completion of their jobs these workers return to their Member State of residence and do not have access to the labour market of the host country. Here too reservations are made for temporary agency workers.[32]

In *Finalarte* the Court held the view that Article 39 TFEU does not apply to posted workers and that the free movement of services should be given precedence.[33]

In 2007 and 2008 the judgments of the European Court of Justice in *Viking*[34] and *Laval*[35] restricted the use of collective bargaining and the right to strike as

---

28 Article 58 TFEU.

29 Case C-113/89, *Rush Portuguesa,* 1990, *ECR* I-1417.

30 Such as the condition to hire staff locally or the obligation to apply for work permits.

31 For a more detailed comment on this judgment, see: H. Verschueren, "Het arrest Rush Portuguesa: een nieuwe wending aan het vrije verkeer van werknemers in het Europese gemeenschapsrecht", *T. Vreemd.* 1990, No 58, 3–12 and *Migrantenrecht* 1990, 187–191.

32 Case C-43/93, *Vander Elst,* 1994, *ECR* I-3803.

33 Case C-49/98, *Finalarte,* 2001, *ECR* I-7831.

34 Case C-438/05, *Viking,* 2007, *ECR* I-10779.

35 Case C-341/05, *Laval,* 2007, *ECR* I-11767.

measures to combat social dumping. The Court stated that the free movement of services[36] had been violated, arguing that this freedom outweighs social aspects.[37]

In *Rüffert*[38] and *Commission v. Luxembourg*[39] legislation aimed at imposing equal or better working conditions for temporarily employed workers was considered to be incompatible with the EU provisions on free movement of services and the Posted Workers Directive.[40] In doing so the Court of Justice tried to reconcile two opposites: free movement of services on the one hand and adequate social protection of workers on the other.[41]

With this case law the Court dissociated itself from the European social model that is based on the protection of the weakest contracting party, i.e. the employee. The Court weighs up the protection of employees and the economic freedoms of the employers; apparently the latter may not be restricted.[42] Most of all, this case law shows that the European construction and the European policies amount to nothing more than the realization of the internal market.

Therefore, we can conclude that over the past years the European internal market has put considerable pressure on the territorial and national application of labour law and social security law. This pressure was mainly due to the free movement of services and the freedom of establishment. The Court of Justice plays a crucial role in this respect.[43]

2.1.2.5. Restrictions on free movement

Free movement is not without restrictions. In this section we will examine legal restrictions as well as restrictions developed in case law.

The TFEU only allows limits to the free movement of services in the case of activities connected with the exercise of official authority (Article 51, former

---

36 The Viking case concerned the freedom of establishment.

37 N. Reich, "Free Movement vs. Social Rights in an Enlarged Union – the *Laval* and *Viking* Cases before the ECJ", *German Law Journal* (2008), 125; G. Orlandini, "Trade Union Rights and Market Freedoms: the European Court of Justice Sets Out the Rules", *Comparative Labor Law & Policy Journal*, 573. In February 2008 John Monks, Secretary General of the European Trade Union Confederation, labelled the Court's judgments in Viking and Laval a licence for social dumping: J. Monks, Presentation to the Employment and Social Affairs Committee of the EP, para. 6, available at: www.etuc.org.

38 Case C-346/06, *Rüffert*, 2008, *ECR* I-1989.

39 Case C-319/06, *Commission v. Luxembourg*, 2008, *ECR* I-458.

40 For some more recent and differently approached comments on the Court's case law, see: S. Prechal and S.A. De Vries, "Viking/Laval en de grondslagen van het interne marktrecht"', *SEW* 2008, 425–440; F. Dorssemont, "De collectieve arbeidsvoorwaarden (van het werkland) en de gedetacheerde werknemers", *AA* 2008, issue 3, 67–104.

41 M. Traest, "De detachering van werknemers in het internationaal privaatrecht na de Europese richtlijn van 16 december 1996", *RW* 1998–99, 1340.

42 H. Verschueren, above n. 3, pp. 173 et seq.; S. Giubboni, above n. 3, pp. 175–176.

43 H. Verschueren, above n. 3, p. 195.

Article 45 TEC) and restrictions on grounds of public order, public safety and public health (Article 52, former Article 46 TEC).[44]

We think it would be useful to have a look at the restrictions on grounds of public safety. According to the study on working conditions in road transport carried out by order of the European Parliament, job demands are among the most problematic issues.[45] According to the study carried out by the ETF between 2008 and 2012 among approximately 1,000 professional lorry drivers, 80% of the non-resident drivers questioned stated that fatigue is a real problem.[46] What is the cause? A number of European professional drivers are employed in Western European countries through letter-box companies, temporary employment agencies or other constructions. Often, they are away from home for weeks in a row, mostly spending the night in their lorries. They take their rest periods and meal breaks near their vehicles or on the roadside. Their basic wages are equal to the basic wages in their country of origin with some supplements. However, this is insufficient to pay for hotel accommodation. It is clear that these working conditions can jeopardize road safety and when public safety is threatened measures may be taken to limit the free movement of services.

In addition to the legal restrictions, there are also restrictions as a result of judgments by the Court of Justice. In its case law the Court established a number of conditions under which additional exceptions to the free movement of services are permitted, more specifically because of a *rule of reason*. This means that the freedom to provide services as one of the basic principles of the EC Treaty can only be limited by arrangements justified by *overriding reasons of public interest* which apply to all persons or undertakings active in the territory of the State concerned, in so far as this interest is not safeguarded by the rules to which the service provider is subject in the Member State where he/she is established.[47]

One of the overriding reasons of general interest recognized by the Court is the protection of the workers.[48] Other objectives that can be invoked to justify restrictions of the free movement of services are the protection of the financial balance of the social security systems and the prevention of unfair competition

---

44 Pursuant to Article 55 EC Treaty these articles apply to the free movement of services.

45 Study on Social and Working Conditions of Road Transport Hauliers of the Directorate Genera for Internal Policies of the European Parliament, Policy Department B: Structural and Cohesion Policies, Transport and Tourism, 2013, available at: www.europarl.europa.eu/RegData/etudes/etudes/join/2013/495855/IPOL-TRAN_ET(2013)495855_EN.pdf.

46 ETF Survey on working and living conditions of non-resident drivers in the EU, available at: www.etf-europe.org/files/extranet/-75/39267/Methodology%20of%20the%204%20year%20ETF%20survey.pdf.

47 Case C-279/80, *Webb*, 1981, *ECR* I-3305, para. 17; Case C-180/89, *Commission v. Italy*, 1989, *ECR* I-709, para. 17; Case C-43/93, *Vander Elst*, 1994, *ECR* I-3803, para. 16; and Case C-272/94, *Guiot*, 1994, *ECR* I-1905, para. 11.

48 Case C-279/80, *Webb*, 1981, *ECR* I-3305, para. 19; Case C-62/81 and C-63/81, *Seco and Desquenne & Giral*, 1981, *ECR* I-223, para. 14; Case C-113/89, *Rush Portuguesa*, 1990, *ECR* I-1417, para. 18; Joined Cases C-369/96 and C-376/96, *Arblade-Leloup*, 1999, *ECR* I-8453, para. 36; and Case C-164/99, *Portugaia*, 2002, *ECR* I-787.

and social dumping.[49] Indeed, in defining and implementing its policies and activities the Union takes into account requirements linked to the promotion of a high level of employment, the guarantee of adequate social protection and the fight against social exclusion as well as a high level of education, training and protection of human health (Article 9 TFEU). In 2006, in *Commission v. Germany*, the Court explicitly expressed its concern about the dangers of social dumping: "as regards the prevention of social dumping the Member States may extend their legislation or collective agreements relating to minimum wages to any person who is employed, even temporarily, within their territory".[50]

However, the case law of the Court of Justice often tips the scales in favour of the EU provisions on free movement. It would seem that the Court's eagerness with regard to the fight against social dumping, not counting a few exceptions, is rather limited. Wage competition is considered to be the driving force of the internal market. This position is criticized in legal doctrine and rightly so.[51]

Finally, the literature also offers a possible avenue with regard to the restrictions on free movement. Verschueren quotes case law of the Court of Justice which indicates the possibility of invoking the free movement of workers, even in situations in which a worker is only temporarily active in another country in the context of the provision of services.[52] Assuming that it would be possible to invoke the free movement of workers and the principle of non-discrimination (Article 45 TFEU) in this matter as well, it would be conceivable

49 F. van Overbeeke, "Het IPR als instrument ter versterking van de positie van de gedetacheerde werknemer in het web van het vrij verkeer", *TSR* 2013, 697; see Article 9 TFEU. See also Case C-438/05, *Viking*, 2007, *ECR* I-10779, para. 77: "the protection of workers is one of the overriding reasons of public interest recognized by the Court". See also Case C-369/96, *Arblade*, 1999, *ECR* I-8453; Case C-165/98, *Mazzoleni*, 2001, *ECR* I-2189. For social dumping as a legitimate interest see: Case C-167/73, *Commission v. France*, 1974, *ECR* I-373; Case C-341/05, *Laval*, 2007, *ECR* I-11767, para. 103; Case C-577/10, *Commission v. Belgium* (www.curia.eu). See also Article 151 TFEU under Social Policy.

50 Case C-244/04, *Commission v. Germany*, 2006, *ECR* I-885, para. 61; H. Verschueren, above n. 3, p. 181.

51 Van Hoek and Houwerzijl commented that looked at from an PIL angle the acceptance of wage competition as the driving force of the internal market is doubtful: A.A.H. Van Hoek and M.S. Houwerzijl, "Loonconcurrentie als motor van de interne markt?", *NTER* 2008, p. 205; see C. Barnard, "Employment rights, free movement under the EC Treaty and the Services Directive", available at: www.etui-rehs.org/en/Headline-issues/Viking-Laval1Rueffert-Luxembourgj2-Articles-in-academic-literature-onthe-judgements; V. Van den Eeckhout, "Internationaal arbeidsrecht gemangeld tussen Europese fundamentele vrijheden", available at: https://openaccess.leidenuniv.nl/bitstream/handle/1887/13815/V%20Van%20Den%20Eeckhout%20-%20Internationaal%20arbeidsrecht%20gemangeld%20tussen%20Europese%20fundamentele%20vrijheden.pdf?sequence=1; V. Van den Eeckhout, "Internationaal arbeidsrecht gemangeld tussen vrij verkeer van personen, vrij verkeer van diensten, vrijheid van vestigen en non-discriminatie. Enkele aantekeningen vanuit ipr-perspectief bij de uitspraken van Viking, Laval, Rüffert, en C./Luxemburg", Working Paper Series: REFGOV-FR-26, 2009, 26.

52 H. Verschueren, above n. 3, pp. 174–177.

to work up to the applicability of rules of the host country which would amount to a territorial application of labour law.

2.2. THE CHARTER OF FUNDAMENTAL RIGHTS OF THE EUROPEAN UNION

In the European Union the protection of fundamental rights is guaranteed at a national level by the constitutional systems of the Member States and at EU level by the Charter of Fundamental Rights of the European Union (the Charter).

Article 1 of the Charter states that human dignity is inviolable and must be respected and protected.[53] Article 31 guarantees all workers the right to healthy, safe and decent working conditions. All workers are entitled to a restriction of the maximum working time and to daily and weekly rest periods as well as to annual paid holidays. These rights are fundamental rights that have to be observed at all times. Ever since the Treaty of Lisbon the Charter has the same legal value as a treaty. The principles of the free movement of workers, the freedom of establishment and the free movement of services must be tested against these fundamental rights. The EU's transport policy must also respect these fundamental rights.

Given the fact that it concerns a downward *Gleichschaltung* of the social rights in the various Member States, the Charter of the Fundamental Rights of the European Union is actually a step backwards compared to the constitutions of the various Member States and the ECHR. However, the Charter does contain the fundamental right of human dignity. This fundamental right is a primary fundamental right and the source and objective of all other fundamental rights. It transcends them, sums them up and can be used in connection with other fundamental rights.[54]

The EU Charter of Fundamental Rights applies to all actions undertaken by the EU institutions. It is the Commission's duty to make sure that its legislative proposals are compatible with the Charter. All EU institutions (especially the European Parliament and the Council) are responsible for the observance of the Charter in the legislative process.

The Charter only applies to the Member States when they implement EU law. If a person is of the opinion that a national authority has violated the Charter in the implementation of EU law, he/she can lodge a complaint with the

53 The preamble already refers to human dignity: "Conscious of its spiritual and moral heritage the Union is founded on the indivisible, universal values of human dignity, freedom, equality and solidarity."

54 G. Maes, *De afdwingbaarheid van sociale grondrechten*, Intersentia, Antwerp 2003, pp. 444 et seq.

Commission, which is authorized to start legal proceedings against the Member State in question.

The Court of Justice has the last word as regards the observance of the treaties, the Charter and EU legislation. It sees to it that these are interpreted and applied in the same manner all over the Union and that the EU institutions and the Member States do what EU law requires them to do.

If citizens or undertakings hold the view that an act by an EU institution with a direct impact on them violates their fundamental rights, they can take their case to the Court of Justice which, in certain circumstances, is authorized to annul such an act. However, a citizen cannot submit a claim against another (legal or natural) person or against a Member State.

2.3. THE RELATION BETWEEN THE INTERNAL MARKET AND THE FUNDAMENTAL SOCIAL RIGHTS

The relationship between free movement and the fundamental social rights is problematic and tense. Quite often the right to free movement seems to take precedence.

The policies and legislation of the European Union were and still are almost completely built on the development of the internal market. Neither social rights nor upward social harmonization in terms of employment and working conditions have been given the same attention.[55]

The fundamental rights as described in the TFEU and the Charter must be observed, even if this means that the principles of free movement must give way.

In the judgments of the European Court of Justice in *Viking*, *Laval*, *Rüffert* and *Commission v. Luxembourg* the Court presents another view. It sets up a hierarchy of norms in which the market freedoms are on top and the fundamental social rights and collective bargaining are relegated to the second place.

Better protection of social rights within the Union is required.[56]

2.4. CONCLUSION

Social dumping is a symptom of the European construction. The TFEU has established a liberalized transport market. The Court of Justice emphasizes the economic freedoms, freedoms which are often at odds with the fundamental

---

55 S. Giubboni, above n. 3, pp. 162–163; F.W. Scharpf, above n. 3, p. 645; H. Verschueren, above n. 3, pp. 167–168.

56 B. Bercusson, "The Trade Union Movement and the European Union: The Judgement Day", *ELJ* 2007, 279; S. Giubboni, above n. 3, p. 182.

social rights. An internal market without equal attention for social rights leads to the practices of social dumping and unfair competition we see today in the transport sector. To deal with these practices an adaptation of the European construction is absolutely necessary. Before offering a number of avenues in this respect, we will discuss the other European rules and regulations that are essential for the road transport sector.

3. OTHER EUROPEAN RULES AND REGULATIONS RELEVANT TO THE ROAD TRANSPORT SECTOR

In the previous section we discussed the way in which Europe has been set up, which position has been given to the fundamental social rights and how this leads to social dumping.

To get a good understanding of the road transport sector it is also necessary to pay attention to private international law, to the trend-setting judgments in *Koelzsch* and *Voogsgeerd* (section 3.1), to Regulation 1071/2009 which lays down the conditions under which transport companies can enter the market (section 3.2), to the cabotage regulations, because these play a decisive role in the functioning of the road transport sector (section 3.3), and to the Posted Workers Directive and the Enforcement Directive (section 3.4).[57] We conclude with a short survey of the material law on working conditions (section 3.5).

3.1. PRIVATE INTERNATIONAL LAW

The advancing liberalization of the transport market has been paving the way for social dumping. The easiest construction is the transfer of registered office so as to avoid higher pay and better working conditions. The following constructions come to mind: an entrepreneur opens a new establishment in another EU country, takes over an existing company in another EU country or even moves the company's main office to another EU country. All these options are possible in the context of the freedom of establishment. But the question is whether these options also offer the possibility of evading the national systems of pay and working conditions in the road transport sector.

Private international law is a key factor in this issue.

To determine which law applies to an international employment relationship or a cross-border employment contract private international law must be

57 Although the relevance of these directives for the transport sector in general is contested, there can be no doubt as to their relevance for cabotage activities and for other sectors in which social dumping practices are prevalent, such as the construction industry, the cleaning sector, etc.

applied.[58] If the parties have not made a choice of law, the law of the country from where the worker habitually carries out his/her job applies.[59] The country where the work is usually carried out is considered not to have changed if the worker carries out his/her job in another country temporarily. However, if the worker does not usually carry out his/her work in the same country, the law of the country in which the company that has engaged the worker is established applies. This second criterion is a subsidiary criterion which, in other words, can only be applied if the worker does not habitually carry out his/her work in the same country. Nonetheless, if it is certain that the employment contract is more closely connected to a country other than the country of habitual employment and/or the country of the establishment that has engaged the worker, the law of that other country must be applied (Article 8 Rome I Regulation).[60] Even if the parties have made a choice of law, this may not have as a consequence that the worker loses the protection he/she enjoys on the basis of the mandatory provisions of the normally applicable law.

In the judgment of the European Court of Justice of 15 March (*Koelzsch*)[61] and the judgment of 15 December 2011 (*Voogsgeerd*)[62] the Rome I Convention was applied to the specific circumstances of the transport sector.[63]

In *Koelzsch*, which relates to road transport, the Court defines the place of habitual employment as the place where or from where the worker performs the major part of his obligations towards his employer. The Court specifies that the national court has to determine first in which State the place is situated from which the worker carries out his transport tasks, receives instructions concerning these activities, organizes his work, and the place where his work tools are situated. Furthermore, the court has to determine where the goods are unloaded and the place to which the employee returns after completion of his tasks. Due regard should be given to the pursuit of adequate protection of the employee as the socially weaker of the contracting parties.

---

58 The following rules of law have to be applied: the European Convention of 19 June 1980 on the law applicable to contractual obligations (Rome I Convention), European Regulation 593/2008 (Rome I Regulation) and the Posted Workers Directive.

59 Compared to the Rome I Convention, the Rome I Regulation had already been extended with the provision that employment contracts are governed by the law of the country where, or failing this, *from where* the employee in performance of the employment contract habitually carries out his/her work. The Rome I Convention only referred to the habitual place of employment.

60 Regulation (EC) 593/2008 of the European Parliament and of the Council on the law applicable to contractual obligations, *OJ L* 2008/177, 6. However, Denmark made reservations with regard to the application of the Rome I Regulation, as a result of which this is not binding for Denmark.

61 Case C-29/10, *Koelzsch*, 2011, *ECR* I-1595.

62 Case C-384/10, *Voogsgeerd*, *NJB* 2012, 126.

63 The Rome I Convention is the predecessor of the Rome I Regulation. The difference between the two instruments is negligible (apart from the codification: "from where"). Therefore the judgments in *Koelzsch* and *Voogsgeerd* are of direct importance for the explanation of the Rome I Regulation.

This judgment confirms that non-resident professional drivers employed by Western European transport companies should receive the pay and working conditions of the country where or from where they usually carry out their work.

On 15 December 2011 the Court of Justice rendered another judgment, this time concerning the shipping industry.[64] In *Voogsgeerd* the Court states that if the findings show that if the place from where the worker carries out his transport tasks and where he receives his instructions is always the same, this place must be considered to be the place where he usually carries out his work within the meaning of Article 6(2)(a) (*Voogsgeerd,* Consideration 39).

In September 2013 the European Court of Justice (Third Chamber) rendered a judgment in *Scheckler* in which the third criterion, i.e. closer ties, was applied.[65] In this case, which does not concern the transport industry, the Court of Justice ruled that Article 6(2) must be interpreted as meaning that even when an employee carries out work in performance of the employment contract habitually, for a lengthy period and without interruption in the same country, the national court may, under the concluding part of this provision, disregard the law of the country where the work is habitually carried out if the circumstances as a whole show that the contract is more closely connected with another country. The Court regards as significant factors suggestive of connection with a particular country, first and foremost the fact that the employee pays taxes and contributions there, relating to the income from his/her activity and the fact that he/she is covered by the social security of that country as well as by the various pension, sickness insurance and invalidity schemes. Furthermore, the national court should consider all the circumstances of the case, such as the criteria used to determine the salary and other working conditions.

This judgment raises a number of questions, to say the least, and does not particularly benefit legal certainty. Indeed, the question is whether this interpretation by the Court of Justice is in keeping with its observations in *Koelzsch* and *Voogsgeerd* and with the principles of the Rome I Convention and the Rome I Regulation, which state that due regard should be paid to the pursuit of adequate protection of the employee as the socially weaker of the contracting parties.[66]

We may conclude that the actual place of habitual employment is often hard to determine, which gives the national court a lot of discretionary power, as a result of which the employee's legal certainty and protection are threatened.[67] Today's private international law does not offer professional drivers sufficient protection. So a different connecting factor is required (section 4.4).

---

64 Case C-384-10, *Voogsgeerd, NJB* 2012, 126.

65 Case C-64/12, *RW* 2013–14, 1035, with comment by F. van Overbeeke, available at: http://eurlex.europa.eu/LexUriServ/LexUriServ.do?uri=CELEX:62012CJ0064:NL:HTML.

66 F. van Overbeeke, above n. 49, pp. 699–751.

67 S. Bouzoumita and H. Storme, *Recente evoluties in het internationaal privaatrecht betreffende arbeidsovereenkomsten,* Sociale Praktijkstudies No 22, Kluwer, 2005, p. 34.

3.2. ACCESS TO THE MARKET IN THE INTERNATIONAL CARRIAGE OF GOODS BY ROADS: REGULATION 1071/2009

European Regulation 1071/2009 should make it harder for entrepreneurs to set up letter-box companies.[68]

The regulation contains common provisions concerning access to the market in the international transport of goods by road in the interest of fair competition.[69] Proper compliance with and reliable monitoring of the conditions governing the admission to the occupation of road transport operator presuppose that companies have an effective and stable establishment. It is the responsibility of the Member State of establishment to verify that a company satisfies, at all times, the conditions laid down in this regulation so as to enable the competent authorities of this State to decide, if necessary, to suspend or withdraw the authorization which allows that company to operate on the market.

Companies engaged in the occupation of road transport operator shall have an effective and stable establishment in a Member State, be of good repute, have appropriate financial standing and have the requisite professional competence.

In order to satisfy the requirement of having an effective and stable establishment in a Member State a company must, first of all, have an establishment situated in that Member State with premises in which it keeps its core business documents, in particular its accounting documents, personnel management documents, documents containing data relating to driving time and rest periods and any other document to which the competent authority must have access in order to verify compliance with the conditions laid down in this regulation. Member States may require that establishments on their territory also have other documents available at their premises at any time. Secondly, once an authorization has been granted, a company must have at its disposal one or more vehicles which are registered or otherwise put into circulation in conformity with the legislation of that Member State, either wholly owned or, for instance, held by a hire-purchase agreement or a hire or leasing contract. In the third place, an undertaking must conduct, effectively and continuously, its operations concerning the vehicle mentioned above with the necessary administrative means and with the appropriate technical equipment and facilities in an operating centre situated in that Member State.[70]

However, this regulation causes two problems.

First of all the regulation does not offer a Member State the possibility of taking action against a Member State which does not observe the obligations of

---

68 Regulation (EC) 1072/2009 of the European Parliament and of the Council of 21 October 2009 on common rules for the international road haulage market.

69 Recital 6 Regulation 1071/2009.

70 Article 5 Regulation 1071/2009.

the regulation. The regulation only instructs the competent authorities of the Member States to work closely together and to offer each other mutual assistance with a view to the application of this regulation.

The second problem is that the various Member States interpret the regulation differently. Some Member States consider an office with wage records to be sufficient; other States take the view that genuine transport activities have to be carried out. Given the wording of Article 5, the latter is in our view the only correct one. Yet, in order to avoid all disputes, this article should be put in more concrete terms (section 4.5).

3.3. CABOTAGE REGULATIONS

Cabotage is the performance of national transport operations on behalf of a third party temporarily carried out by a road transport operator of a certain Member State in another Member State without having a registered office or other establishment in that Member State and which is not part of combined transport as defined in Directive 92/106/EEC.[71] A cabotage operation is for instance a journey from Leuven to Brussels by a driver employed by a Bulgarian company who is not part of combined transport.

The liberalization of international road haulage has been completed. However, as regards cabotage, this is not yet the case. The first step was the introduction of the Community cabotage quota in 1989, on the basis of which the Member States were allowed to issue cabotage authorizations, within the quota annually allocated to them, to transport operators with a transport authorization established in their country.[72] In 1993 the Council determined that cabotage had to be free by 1 July 1998 and that all restrictions on the basis of nationality or establishment had to be suspended.

So far this is not the case. Cabotage continues to be subject to restrictions.

The concern about and the reason for the restrictions are caused by the fact that transport operators from Member States with a low level of working conditions offer their services for the national transport of goods in Member States with higher social costs and by the fact that transport operators from the

71 Council Regulation No 3118/93 of 25 October 1993 and Regulation (EC) No 1072/2009 of the European Parliament and of the Council of 21 October 2009. The "host Member State" is a Member State where a transport operator is active, but which is not his/her Member State of establishment.

72 Regulation 4059/89 of 21 December 1989, *OJ L* 1989, 390, 3. This regulation was declared null and void but the Court of Justice ruled that on the basis of Article 174 EEC Treaty the consequences of the annulled regulation continue to apply until the Council, after consultation with the European Parliament, has decided on a new regulation, see A.J. Braakman, "Juridische actualiteiten in verband met cabotage" in the syllabus of the seminar "*De transportsector in een veranderend Europa*", 3 June 1993, Kamer van Koophandel en Fabrieken voor Rotterdam en Beneden Maas, pp. 5–7.

latter set up businesses in a Member State with lower social costs while at the same continuing to offer their services in the Member State of origin. As to the question whether that way they can avoid the working conditions of the country where they provide their services, we refer to the part on private international law.

In the interest of a smooth and flexible realization of a common transport policy, and because of the continuing lack of harmonization of the road transport market, a temporary cabotage arrangement was provided for.[73]

The objective of Regulation 1072/2009 was the harmonization of the rules on cabotage all over the EU. It was adopted at the time that a lot of changes took place on the EU's international goods transport market, mainly as a result of the expansion of the EU in 2004, which opened the gates for transport operators from new Member States – albeit with some restrictions.[74] The two main provisions are, first, the introduction of the rule that in the seven days following the international transport operation, at most three cabotage operations are allowed, and, second, the harmonization of the documents which the driver has to have in his/her possession during the cabotage operation in order to confirm the legitimacy of the operation.[75]

The European Union's objective continues to be the completion of the internal market; in other words, Europe wants to remove the restrictions on cabotage transport.[76]

---

73 Regulation (EC) 1072/2009 of the European Parliament and of the Council of 21 October 2009 on common rules for the international road haulage market, Recital 4–5.

74 In 2009 (and in 2012 for Romania and Bulgaria) these restrictions were cancelled.

75 The EU legislation preceding this regulation (in the form of Regulation (ECC) 3118/93) already contained a number of provisions on cabotage, but not all issues had been sufficiently specified (e.g. what was meant by the statement that cabotage had to be temporary?) and led to different interpretations at the national level. An attempt was made to solve these problems via a number of provisions in Regulation 1072/2009.

76 White Paper of 28 March 2011, "Roadmap to a Single European Transport Area – Towards a competitive and resource efficient transport system": "Europe wants to: – review the market situation of road freight transport as well as the degree of convergence on, among others, road user charges, social and safety legislation, transposition and enforcement of the legislation in the Member States, with a view to further opening road transport markets. In particular, the elimination of restrictions on cabotage; – review the rules on the tachograph to make it more cost-effective, give access to the EU register on road transport undertakings to police and enforcement officers when they carry out roadside checks; harmonize sanctions for infringement to EU rules on professional transport; harmonize training of enforcement officers; – adapt the legislation on weight and dimension to new circumstances, technologies and needs (e.g. weight of batteries, better aerodynamic performance), and to make sure it facilitates intermodal transport and the reduction of overall energy consumption and emissions. And at the same time: promote quality jobs and working conditions: Social code for mobile road transport workers – encourage and support the dialogue between social partners in view of an agreement on a social code for mobile road transport workers, addressing also the problem of disguised self-employment. And also; – conduct an appraisal of the sectoral social dialogue processes taking place in the various segments of the transport sector to the end of improving social dialogue and facilitating its effectiveness; – ensure employee involvement, in particular through European Works Councils, in transnational

The analysis of market data shows that since the expansion of 2004 considerable changes have occurred in the EU cabotage market. Overall, the proportion of cabotage operations with vehicles from one of the EU12 Member States increased from 12% in 2007 to almost 40% in 2011. In this respect, there are two important developments. First, an increasing number of companies from the EU15 Member States have resorted to "flagging out" in order to benefit from the profitable differences in labour costs and to regain their competitiveness. Second, companies from the EU12 Member States have made greater use of the opportunities offered by cabotage because they can offer cheaper alternatives to European consignees looking for a reduction in costs.[77]

At the latest by the end of 2013 the Commission had to write a report on the state of the EU road transport market. It finally did so in April 2014.[78] One of the Commission's findings was that there are few reported infringements of the cabotage provisions and that, in the long term, measures to limit cabotage (e.g. a smartphone application to trace lorries registered abroad) would undermine the internal market and its efficiency. We do not agree with this point of view. The table in the 2013 report on the working and living conditions of professional drivers of the European Parliament clearly shows that infringements of cabotage rules are a real problem.[79] If the cabotage restrictions are abolished there is a real chance of more social dumping. Some Member States (among which Belgium, France and Germany) take the same view. On 5 December 2013 they wrote a letter to the European Commission stating that at present there should be no further liberalization.

3.4. THE POSTED WORKERS AND ENFORCEMENT DIRECTIVES

From the Court's case law it was not always possible to infer for certain to what extent Member States were allowed to apply their national labour law to posted employees of service providers established abroad.

---

companies in the sector; – address quality of work in all transport modes, with respect to, notably, training, certification, working conditions and career development, with a view to creating quality jobs, developing the necessary skills and strengthening the competitiveness of EU transport operators."

77 Report on Development and Implementation of EU Road Cabotage, Directorate General for Internal Policies, Policy Department B: Structural and Cohesion Policies, Transport and Tourism, 2013, 91 p.

78 Report made by the Commission in April 2014.

79 Table 2: Issues Identified by Stakeholders as Requiring Future Legislative Action with Respect to Social and Working Conditions in the Road Freight Transport Sector. Source: Social and Working Conditions of Road Transport Hauliers, European Parliament, 2013, Report from the Commission to the European Parliament and the Council on the State of the Union Road Transport Market, 14 April 2014, 18.

In 1996 an attempt was made to remedy this by adopting the Posted Workers Directive,[80] in which a balance between the free movement of services, fair competition and the protection of workers was put forward.[81] By the law of 5 March 2002 the Posted Workers Directive was transposed into Belgian legislation.[82]

The Posted Workers Directive contains both a definition of posting (Article 1(1) and (3)) and a definition of posted worker (Article 2). These concepts have to be combined to determine the scope of the directive. For the purposes of the directive a "posted worker" means a worker who, for a certain period, works on the territory of a Member State which is not the State where he/she usually works.

The Posted Workers Directive applies to undertakings established in a Member State which, in the framework of the transnational provisions of services, find themselves in one of the three situations defined in the directive.[83] In these three situations the service provider will have to observe a "hard core" of employment terms and conditions in the Member State where the work is carried out.[84]

This directive is supposed to be a compromise between the service providers' interests in terms of competitiveness and the protection of workers. However, the Posted Workers Directive clearly "breathes" the free movement of services.[85] The Court of Justice has seen to it that the application of labour law to posted workers fits within the internal market and the free movement of services. The

---

80 Directive 96/71 of the European Parliament and of the Council of 16 December 1996 concerning the posting of workers in the framework of the provision of services, *OJ L* 1997/18, 1 (Posted Workers Directive).

81 See the Commission's first proposal of 1991, *OJ C* 1991/225, 6.

82 An employer employing in Belgium a posted worker shall, for the work done by said worker, comply with the working, pay and employment conditions as laid down in legal, administrative or conventional provisions subject to penal law, among which collective agreements that have been declared to be generally binding.

83 Article 1(3) Posted Workers Directive:
"– post workers to the territory of a Member State on their account and under their direction, *under a contract concluded between the undertaking making the posting and the party for whom the services are intended*, operating in that Member State, provided there is an employment relationship between the undertaking making the posting and the worker during the period of posting; or
– post workers to *an establishment or to an undertaking owned by the group* in the territory of a Member State, provided there is an employment relationship between the undertaking making the posting and the worker during the period of posting; or
– *being a temporary employment undertaking or placement agency, hire out a worker to a user undertaking* in the territory of a Member State, provided there is an employment relationship between the temporary employment undertaking or placement agency and the worker during the period of posting."

84 Article 3(1) Posted Workers Directive.

85 Recital 5 Posted Workers Directive: M.S. Houwerzijl, *De detacheringsrichtlijn. Over de achtergrond, inhoud en implementatie van Richtlijn 96/71/EG*, PhD thesis, Tilburg University, 2005, pp. 357–358.

directive can lead to social dumping and competitive advantages; in a number of cases it reduces the social protection of workers.[86]

Now, the question is whether the Posted Workers Directive applies to the transport sector.

First, the Posted Workers Directive does not exclude international transport from its scope.[87] So, if the conditions of posting are fulfilled, the Posted Workers Directive applies.

This does not alter the fact that it is harder to apply the directive, which has mainly been written with the construction industry in mind, to international transport. Indeed, the definition in the Posted Workers Directive concerns a worker who, during a certain period, works on the territory of a Member State. Professional drivers on the other hand work on the territory of several Member States. So, the question is whether "on the territory of a Member State" must be interpreted as strictly on the territory or as the place where or from where a worker starts working. We take the view that it can be interpreted as "where or from where" and refer in this respect to the Court's interpretation in *Mulox*,[88] *Rutten*[89] and *Weber*,[90] the case law of which has been transposed into the Brussels I *bis* Regulation, as well as to the Court's interpretation in *Koelzsch* of the Rome I Convention which has been transposed into the Rome I Regulation.[91]

As stated in Recital 17 of Regulation 1072/2009 it is clear that the provisions of the Posted Workers Directive do apply to transport companies carrying out cabotage operations.

Both for international transport and for cabotage the rule is that if the Posted Workers Directive does not apply, professional drivers fall back on the Rome I Regulation.

The number of postings has increased drastically, especially since the entry of ten new Member States on 1 May 2004. In its nearly 20 years of existence the enforcement of the Posted Workers Directive has continued to be problematic. The fact that the posting system is not really monitored is one of the reasons for the occurrence of disguised postings. This is for instance the case when a worker is not usually employed in the sending Member State but is "directly" posted to the host Member State.

86 H. Verschueren, above n. 3, p. 198.

87 The only category to which this directive does not apply is the seagoing personnel of merchant navy undertakings (Article 1(2)).

88 Case C-125/92, *Mulox*, 1993, *ECR* I-04075.

89 Case C-383/95, *Rutten*, 1993, *ECR* I-00057.

90 Case C-37/00,*Weber*, 2003, *ECR* I-03573.

91 The place where the worker habitually works also means the place "from where" he/she habitually works.

The new Enforcement Directive should improve this and ensure better enforcement of the EU rules.[92] The Member States have two years, until 18 June 2016, to transpose the directive into national legislation.

The directive does not contain new rules – the basic principle continues to be respect for the "hard core of working conditions" – but aims at better enforcement, inter alia, by reinforcing the social inspections. The new Enforcement Directive is intended to improve, promote and strengthen the practical exercise, application and enforcement of the Posted Workers Directive. Furthermore, the directive offers measures to prevent abuse and circumvention as well as safeguards for the protection of the posted workers' rights (Article 1(1)).

Without going into detail we would like to discuss two conditions of this Enforcement Directive which seem important to prevent abuse in posting.

The first condition is the definition of the temporary character, which is inherent to the concept of posting, on the basis of a non-exhaustive list (Article 4). The second is the condition that the employer is genuinely established in the Member State from where the posting takes place.[93] This means that an undertaking in the sending Member State has to genuinely carry out substantial activities other than purely internal management and/or administrative activities, which should render it harder to set up letter-box companies. The competent authorities must make an overall assessment of all factual elements.[94] Both conditions have to be verified by the competent authorities of the host Member State, in close collaboration with the Member State of establishment.

The control measures and obligation of information are an improvement of the rights of posted workers. However, in our view the Enforcement Directive, which is the result of a compromise, still leaves too much room for interpretation. The competent institutions of the Member States will have to collaborate as provided for in Articles 6 and 8. Sanctions against Member States which do not cooperate or do not cooperate sufficiently have not been provided for.

---

92 Directive 2014/67/EU of the European Parliament and of the Council of 15 May 2014 on the enforcement of Directive 96/71/EC concerning the posting of workers in the framework of the provision of services and amending Regulation (EU) 1024/2012 on administrative cooperation through the Internal Market Information Regulation (IMI Regulation), *OJ L* 2014/159, 11.

93 A. Defossez, "Le dépassement de la question du dumping social: une condition nécessaire à une meilleure application de la directive détachement", *TSR* 2014, I, 121.

94 Such as the place where the undertaking has its registered office and administration, uses office space, pays taxes and social security contributions and, where applicable, in accordance with national law has a professional licence or is registered with the chambers of commerce or professional bodies; the place where posted workers are recruited and from which they are posted; the law applicable to the contracts concluded by the undertaking with its workers, on the one hand, and with the clients, on the other; the place where the undertaking performs its substantial business activity and where it employs administrative staff; the number of contracts performed and/or the size of the turnover realized in the Member State of establishment, taking into account the specific situation of, inter alia, newly established undertakings and SMEs.

In any case, as the basic principles are not altered and only the "hard core" provisions of the host country apply, it remains to be seen whether the Enforcement Directive will be sufficient.

3.5. MATERIAL LAW APPLICABLE

Although the liberalization of goods transport has made a lot of headway, the harmonization of the social rules for this sector has not made the same progress. Still, some common rules have been introduced with regard to driving time and rest periods,[95] the minimum level of training for road transport drivers[96] and requirements with regard to the driving licence. These are some of the main features.

The following European rules and regulations apply specifically to road transport.

In Regulation 561/2006 common rules for remuneration per kilometre and driving time and rest periods for professional drivers have been determined.[97] This regulation applies to all professional drivers driving vehicles of more than 3.5 tons in the case of international transport, cross-border transport and cabotage.

Mobile drivers are excluded from the original Working Time Directive.[98] They are subject to Directive 2002/15/EC on the organization of the working time of persons who carry out mobile activities in road transport. These specific provisions regarding working time are intended to guarantee the safety of the transport and the health and safety of the persons concerned. This directive has to be transposed into national legislation and applies to all professional drivers with lorries weighing more than 3.5 tons, in the case of international transport, cross-border transport and cabotage. For drivers of vehicles weighing less than 3.5 tons the horizontal Working Time Directive 2003/88/EC applies.[99]

For common rules on paid holidays, non-established professional drivers can only resort to the Posted Workers Directive and the national transposition law

---

95 First regulation: Regulation 3820/85 of 20 December 1985 on the harmonization of certain social legislation relating to road transport and Regulation 3821/85 of 20 December 1985 on recording equipment in road transport, see *OJ L* 1985/370.

96 Directive 76/914 of 16 December 1976 on the minimum level of training for some road transport drivers, *OJ L* 1976/357, 36; Directive 89/684 of 21 December 1989 on vocational training for certain drivers of vehicles carrying dangerous goods by road, *OJ L* 1989/398, 33.

97 Regulation (EC) 561/2006 on the harmonization of certain social legislation relating to road transport and amending Regulations (EEC) 3821/85 and (EC) 2135/98 and repealing Council Regulation (EEC) 3820/85.

98 Council Directive 93/104/EC of 23 November 1993 concerning certain aspects of the organization of working time.

99 Directive 2003/88/EC of the European Parliament and of the Council of 4 November 2003 concerning certain aspects of the organization of working time.

of the country where the driver is posted (this can be the Member State where the driver usually carries out his/her activities) and only when this concerns cabotage. The Rome I Regulation applies to international transport, cross-border transport as well as to cabotage.

Finally, there are common rules for the training of non-established professional drivers. These rules are included in Directive 2003/59/EC and in the transposition in national legislation of the country where the driver is established. This directive applies to all transport operations by professional drivers of lorries weighing more than 3.5 tons.

3.6. CONCLUSION

International transport is completely liberalized only cabotage is still subject to restrictions. The harmonization of social legislation in road transport has not made a lot of progress, as a result of which professional drivers in the Member States find themselves in an unequal competitive position.[100] Some transport companies use the liberalization and the unequal competitiveness to underprice in the field of working conditions, which are still very much nationally oriented, and set up cross-border constructions. These constructions do have to comply with the conditions of the Establishment Regulation. The question as to whether constructions make it possible to skirt national legislation is answered by private international law and the Posted Workers Directive.

4. SOME AVENUES TO COMBAT SOCIAL DUMPING IN ROAD TRANSPORT

In this last section we would like to present a few avenues that could stop social dumping in road transport. The basis is the problem of the European construction. The internal market in Europe has been leading to more competition between companies and countries. In combination with the further expansion of the European Union, this is the main cause of social dumping practices.[101] To deal with these practices, above all an adaptation of this European construction is required.

---

100 Not only has the harmonization of social legislation made little progress, at the fiscal level there is not much harmonization either. So in terms of taxes too the transport operators in the various Member States are faced with unequal competitiveness.

101 In a policy study we developed 25 measures against social dumping, both at the European level and the national level, J. Buelens and L. Michielsen, "25 Measures against social dumping", 2014, available at: www.btb-abvv.be/index.php?option=com_content&view=article&id=2998:witboek-25-maatregelen-tegen-sociale-dumping&catid=31:wegvervoer-en-logistiek22&Itemid=202&lang=nl.

Our first proposal is the upward harmonization of the social and fiscal laws of the Member States. This will lead to fair(er) competitiveness among undertakings (section 4.1). In today's Europe this has far from been reached, but exactly for this reason we consider it necessary to emphasize this. The second avenue concerns the strengthening of the fundamental social rights in the European construction (section 4.2). Social dumping puts the position of drivers, both Eastern European and others in the EU, under pressure. Their fundamental social rights do have to be respected. Thirdly, we suggest that the cabotage rules be made more severe. We, as well as some Member States and the European employers' and employees' organizations, are convinced that at present further liberalization should be avoided (section 4.3). Fourthly, a new connecting factor in private international law is needed (section 4.4), and finally, better monitoring is required with regard to the genuine application of European Regulation 1071/2009 (section 4.5).

4.1. TOWARDS AN UPWARD HARMONIZATION OF THE VARIOUS SOCIAL AND FISCAL LAWS OF THE MEMBER STATES

The differences in social and fiscal law in the EU countries are huge. The opening up of the market leads to social dumping and unfair competition because companies set up businesses in countries with weaker social and fiscal legislation. One way to combat this would be the upward harmonization of social and fiscal legislation. This would put an end to unfair competition.[102]

As mentioned before, the Union can only intervene in areas that do not fall under its exclusive power, such as in the field of social law, if and in so far as the objectives of the possible intervention cannot be realized satisfactorily by the Member States themselves. Social dumping is a transnational phenomenon. If the Member States fail to offer a satisfactory response, the Union can interfere.

4.2. THE FUNDAMENTAL SOCIAL RIGHTS MUST BE REINFORCED

As explained above, human dignity is inviolable and must be respected and protected at all times. Apart from this, all workers are entitled to healthy, safe and decent working conditions. These fundamental rights have to be observed, even if this means that the principles of free movement have to give way. Another view would be contrary to the Charter of Human Rights of the European Union. However, in practice the Charter does not seem to be sufficient

102 Techniques to achieve harmonization are described by S. Giubboni, above n. 3, p. 161.

for the protection of workers and therefore should be improved by adding a social progress clause to the European treaties as well as by a fundamental rights test.

4.2.1. Social progress clause

As suggested by the European Trade Union Federation, a social progress clause, in the form of a protocol added to the European treaties, could be an improvement. This protocol, with the same legal value as the treaties, should make it clear that the fundamental social rights have precedence over the economic freedoms.[103]

4.2.2. Fundamental rights test

Secondary EU law (regulations and directives) should always be preceded by a fundamental rights test.[104] That way it would be possible to find out whether or not this legislation respects the fundamental rights.

4.3. NO FURTHER LIBERALIZATION OF CABOTAGE RIGHTS AND HARSHER CABOTAGE RULES

The first priority of the European Community was the establishment of a common transport market, in other words free movement of services and the opening up of the transport markets (under a separate title "Transport", Article 90 et seq. TFEU, *supra*). As far as international goods transport is concerned, the liberalization is completed. As for cabotage, this is not yet the case. The existing restrictions in terms of cabotage have to be preserved and should be developed further.

4.3.1. No further liberalization

The realization of a European internal transport space is the ultimate objective of the EU.[105] However, as long as there is no harmonization of social legislation, fiscal legislation and labour law, the liberalization of cabotage rights can only lead to more social dumping. So, as said before, the restrictions must be

---

103 www.etuc.org/documents/achieving-social-progress-single-market-proposals-protection-fundamental-social-rightsand#.VBf78tkayc0.

104 Such a test already exists, e.g. impact assessment.

105 Report from the Commission to the European Parliament and the Council on the State of the Union Road Transport Market, COM (2014) 222 final, 14 April 2014, available at: http://ec.europa.eu/transport/modes/road/news/com(2014)-222_en.pdf.

maintained. The sector itself is no longer asking for further liberalization. In joint declarations on 7 December 2012 and 17 March 2012 the employees' organization, the European Transport Workers Federation (ETF), and the employers' organization, the International Road Transport Union (IRU), opposed further liberalization of the transport market as long as there is no harmonization of fiscal, social and enforcement rules and regulations.

4.3.2. Harsher cabotage rules

Harsher cabotage rules can counter social dumping. The cabotage rules could be made harsher in three ways.

The current restriction of cabotage operations to a maximum of three in seven days does not apply to combined transport.[106] This means that when goods are supplied by sea or railroad within a radius of 150 km, road transport by any transport company of the EU can be carried out without restrictions. This can lead to social dumping and unfair competition in national transport. Therefore we suggest cabotage restrictions for combined transport as well.[107]

Regulation 1072/2009 provides for a "temporary cabotage regulation" as long as the harmonization of the road transport market has not been completed. Finland has invoked the "temporary basis" of the regulation and laid down in law that non-resident professional drivers in Finland are only allowed a maximum of three transport operations in seven days and ten in a period of three months after termination of the first transport. The new Finnish legislation is the most stringent one in the entire EU.[108] Other Member States should adapt their legislation in that vein.

Our third proposal in this context is the obligation for professional drivers to return to their country of origin after three operations in a certain Member State. In that way, the tactics of transport companies to temporarily send their drivers across the border after three operations in a certain Member State, only to use them for three new transport operations in the same Member State, will be made useless.

---

106 Council Directive 92/106/EC of 7 December 1992 on the establishment of common rules for certain types of combined transport of goods between Member States.

107 In Belgian legislation the restrictions on cabotage also apply to combined transport, Royal Decree of 10 August 2009 establishing the conditions under which transport operators established on the territory of another Member State of the European Union or the European Economic Area are allowed access to national road transport in Belgium.

108 The Finnish government published the new legislation on road transport on 11 April 2013. The European Commission has initiated an infringement procedure against Finland.

4.4. NEW CONNECTING FACTOR IN PRIVATE INTERNATIONAL LAW

When performing the same work, drivers have to receive the same pay and social protection. The legal translation of this "slogan" can be found in Article 8 of the Rome I Regulation: the applicable law is the law of the country of habitual employment or of the country from where the worker usually carries out his/her work, a rule which should be reinforced and complied with.

From the case law of the Court of Justice we can infer that the Court adheres to a broad interpretation of the place where the worker usually carries out his/her work, so that there is little room for the application of the forum of the hiring establishment. This choice is made with a view to the protection of the worker. Then again, it is often difficult to determine in concrete terms what the place of usual employment is, as a result of which the national court has a lot of discretionary power, thus threatening the worker's legal position and protection.[109]

Today's private international law does not give professional drivers enough protection. So another connecting factor is required. At the very least Article 8 of the Rome I Regulation should be developed further, for instance by including the elements supplied in *Koelzsch* in this regulation. It could, for instance, be made clear that in case of doubt the interpretation offering the worker the highest degree of social protection has to be chosen.

4.5. BETTER MONITORING OF THE APPLICATION OF EUROPEAN REGULATION 1071/2009

This regulation allows Member States to withdraw transport authorizations if companies do not observe the conditions of establishment. The regulation should be implemented in that vein and the Member States have to check this.

Member States shall order separate checks to verify whether or not a company meets the conditions governing admission to the occupation of road transport operator whenever the Commission so requests in duly motivated cases. They shall inform the Commission of the results of such checks and of the measures taken after it has been established that the company no longer fulfils the requirements laid down in this regulation. If a Member State needs information about a transport company in another Member State, it may send the Commission a request to have a check carried out in the Member State concerned. The Commission must see to it that this check is effectively carried out. The reports which the Member States have to provide and which are referred to in the regulation can be applied for at the Commission.

---

109 S. Bouzoumita and H. Storme, above n. 67, p. 34.

Pursuant to the regulation the competent authorities of the Member States shall work closely together and offer each other mutual assistance with a view to the application of this regulation. Penalties for Member States in the case of non-compliance with the rules are not provided for. We propose to have sanctions included in the regulation.

If cooperation between the inspection agencies is impossible or if the report of such an agency seems to be contradictory to reality, the inspection agencies of a certain Member State itself could conduct their own investigation in another Member State in order to map out the actual reality, to find out whether a transport company is genuinely established there and to examine whether or not the legal conditions are observed.[110] The regulation should include the Member States' right to check whether or not other Member States are in compliance with its rules.

If it is apparent that the European Commission is not monitoring the specifications of the regulations and is failing to meet its obligations, it should be possible to take action against the Commission.

4.6. CONCLUSION

Social dumping in road transport can be dealt with by all kinds of measures. We have proposed measures at the European level that could contribute to the improvement of the occupation of driver and of the transport sector in general, both of which are at present faced with a downward trend of fierce competition.

5. CONCLUSION

The transport sector is a classic example of the functioning of the European Union and its liberalized transport market.

We have tried to give a survey of the European rules and regulations that have the biggest impact on the issue of social dumping.

The economic freedoms and the liberalization of the market, the extension of the European Union without equal attention for the social aspects and without strong enforcement measures have led to the existence of transnational transport companies looking for the lowest wages. This tendency was/is bound to lead to social dumping practices and unfair competition.

Within today's Europe professional drivers are not always guaranteed a decent position. Yet human dignity is one of the European Union's fundamental rights, a right which cannot be shoved aside just like that by the principles of the internal market.

110 In the event of a dispute the court has discretionary power regarding the evidence.

CHAPTER 4
THE TERRITORIAL APPLICATION OF LABOUR LAW IN THE EU INTERNAL MARKET
On Legal Rules and Economic Interests

Herwig VERSCHUEREN*

1. INTRODUCTION

The European Union distinguishes itself in the first place by its internal market which guarantees the free movement of goods, services, capital and labour (Articles 26–66 TFEU). As regards labour migration, the EU internal market makes it possible for employees to go and work in other Member States or to be posted there by their employers, in the context of the freedom to provide services across the border. The internal market also influences the definition of the territorial scope of national labour law, in particular when there is a cross-border aspect. Moreover, the increasing occurrence of cross-border elements is an unavoidable consequence of the growing European market integration. As a result there can be circumstances in which work carried out on the territory of a certain Member State is not necessarily subject to that Member State's labour law. These restrictions on the application of the host Member State's labour legislation on its own territory undeniably puts pressure on the level of protection in this Member State. In the same vein, these restrictions offer employers from sending Member States the possibility of taking competitive advantage of the differences in employment protection and costs.

This chapter looks into the question of to what extent European internal market law has influenced the territorial application of labour law. First we will give an outline of the origins of the principle that labour law continues to be a matter of national competence (section 2). Subsequently, we will examine the European rules and case law relevant for the definition of the territorial scope

* Professor of International and European Social Law at the University of Antwerp.

of national labour law (section 3). This includes the legislation on the freedom of movement for workers, the rules of private international law (PIL) as well as the case law of the European Court of Justice (CJEU) regarding the freedom to provide of services. We will pay special attention to the meaning of Posted Workers Directive 96/71 and analyse how this Directive and the case law of the Court of Justice relating to this are at the crossroads of legal rules and economic interests. Finally, we will draw some conclusions on the ensuing competition between workers in the European internal market (section 4).

2. IN PRINCIPLE LABOUR LAW CONTINUES TO BE A MATTER OF NATIONAL COMPETENCE

At the start of the European integration in the 1950s labour law was deliberately left out of the European sphere of competence. The EEC Treaty of 1957 hardly paid any attention to social law and social policy in general. The focus was on the establishment of a common European market with the four freedoms (goods, persons, services and capital) and competition policy as the cornerstone. The idea was that the increase of productivity as a result of the creation of a common market would automatically lead to the improvement of the living and working conditions and that therefore the EEC only had to be awarded few, if any, powers in terms of social law.[1] This starting point also complied with the Member States' wish to decide for themselves how to deal with social matters with due attention to the characteristics of their own social and political structures.

This is called "*embedded liberalism*":[2] freeing the market was considered to be the responsibility of the international and/or supranational level. However, this free market was embedded in social policy and social law schemes that were to remain the exclusive right of the national states. The Member States retained the authority to compensate for possible negative effects of the internal market through their social legislation. This is one of the elements that legitimized the creation of the European internal market. Incidentally, it was expected that through the functioning of the common market the Member States would be able to boost their social protection.[3]

Now, more than 50 years later, we know that it did not exactly go that way. This is not the place to analyse the manner in which the relationship between

1 See in particular Art. 117 EEC Treaty.

2 S. Guibboni, *Social Rights and Market Freedom in the European Constitution. A Labour Law Perspective*, Cambridge University Press, Cambridge 2006, pp. 29 et seq.

3 S. Deakin, "The Lisbon Treaty, the *Viking* and *Laval* Judgments and the Financial Crisis: In Search of New Foundations for Europe's 'Social Market Economy'", in: N. Bruun, K. Lörcher and I. Schömann (eds.), *The Lisbon Treaty and Social Europe*, Hart, Oxford 2012, pp. 21–23.

the internal market and social law has evolved at political and legal levels.[4] But in summary we could say that the economic integration of the Member States through the internal market has most certainly had an impact on practically all fields of the legislation and policy of the Member States and that territorially and nationally conceived social law has not escaped this influence. Through so-called "negative integration", which, among other things, aimed at the removal of obstacles to the free movement of persons and services, social legislation came under pressure. Social legislation was regarded by the Court of Justice as a possible obstacle to free movement.[5] The European institutions, and especially the Court of Justice, have been trying to find a balance between the economic market freedoms, which were granted the status of "fundamental rights",[6] and the employment protection in the Member States' national law. In doing so the social dimension was pushed into a subordinate and defensive role, which is clearly illustrated in the much-discussed judgments by the Court of Justice in *Viking* and *Laval*.[7]

Despite the fact that the Member States' labour law has ended up in the economic and social context of the European internal market, the European legislature itself has only intervened in this matter to a limited extent. The small repertory of European employment rules and regulations is a result of the limited powers granted by the European treaties to the European legislature[8] as well as of the absence of a political consensus to make ample use of these powers. It is still a matter of what has been described by Scharf as the "constitutional asymmetry" within the EU between the economic objectives and internal market law, on the

4 For an extensive analysis of this history, with footnote references to the relevant literature see S. Guibboni, above n. 2. See also: C. Barnard, *EU Employment Law*, Oxford University Press, Oxford 2012, pp. 3–45 and B. Bercusson, *European Labour Law*, Cambridge University Press, Cambridge 2009, pp. 101–125.

5 See about the relation between the European market integration and national social law among others: D. Ashiagbor, "Embedding Trade Liberalization in Social Policy: Lessons from the European Union?", *Comparative Labour Law and Policy Journal* 2011, 373–404; C. Barnard, above n. 4, pp. 35–45 and 189–251; P. Craig, *The Lisbon Treaty. Law, Politics, and Treaty Reform*, Oxford University Press, Oxford 2012, pp. 287–329; S. Deakin, "Regulatory competition after *Laval*", in: C. Barnard (ed.), *The Cambridge Yearbook of European Legal Studies*, Vol. 10, 2007–2008, Hart, Oxford 2008, pp. 581–609; S. Guibboni, above n. 2, pp. 79–81; S. Leibfried, "Social Policy. Left to the Judges and the Markets?", in: H. Wallace et al. (eds.), *Policy-Making in the European Union*, Oxford University Press, Oxford 2010, pp. 253–281; F. Rödl, "The Labour Constitution", in: A. von Bogdandy and J. Bast, *Principles of European Constitutional Law*, Hart, Oxford 2010, pp. 624–657; and F. Scharf, "The asymmetry of European integration, or why the EU cannot be a 'social market economy'", *Socio-Economic Review*, 2010, 221–223.

6 See, inter alia, Case C-55/94, *Gebhard*.

7 Case C-438/05, *Viking* and Case C-341/05, *Laval*.

8 However, these powers were gradually developed further, in particular by the Maastricht Treaty of 1992 and the Treaty of Amsterdam of 1996. For the present state of affairs see among others: K. Lörcher, "Social Competences", in: N. Bruun, K. Lörcher and I. Schömann (eds.), *The Lisbon Treaty and Social Europe*, Hart, Oxford 2012, pp. 165–234.

one hand, and the social objectives and social law, on the other.[9] This has led, among other things, to the fact that at the European level economic objectives continue to be the dominant ones and influence and restrict the Member States' social law and social policy.

Still, the European legislation that has been developed over the past decades should not be ignored. It is not our intention to analyse this development in depth in this contribution, but we do want to state that in a number of fields this legislation has produced a far-reaching form of harmonization, such as in the matter of the ban on discrimination, health and safety in the workplace, and in other fields harmonization, albeit less thorough, through minimum standards, e.g. with regard to working hours, restructuring of undertakings and the rights of workers with atypical employment contracts. However, as regards other essential elements of both individual and collective labour law, national law has kept its leading role.

In the following section we will analyse the impact of EU law on the territorial application of national labour law and the ensuing regulatory competition within the borders of a single Member State, a situation which may lead to social competition between workers active there.

3. THE TERRITORIAL APPLICATION OF LABOUR LAW IN CROSS-BORDER SITUATIONS

3.1. PRINCIPLE: FREE MOVEMENT OF WORKERS

Social competition in terms of labour law may occur within a Member State, in particular when the job in question has a cross-border aspect. However, this was not the initial intention given the fact that the original Article 48 EEC (now Article 45 TFEU) stated very clearly that the free movement of workers within the Union entailed the abolition of any discrimination on grounds of nationality between the Member States' workers in terms of employment, pay and other working conditions.

This principle means that migrating workers are entitled to the same pay and working conditions in the Member State where they work as those applicable to that Member State's own citizens. This prohibition of discrimination on grounds of nationality was also explicitly included in Article 7 Regulation 1612/68[10] (now replaced by Article 7 Regulation 492/2011)[11] which, for the application of this

---

9 F. Scharf, "The European Social Model: Coping with the Challenges of Diversity", *Journal of Common Market Studies*, 2002, 645 et seq.

10 Regulation (EEC) 1612/68 of the Council of 25 October 1968 on freedom of movement within the Community, *OJ L* 1968/257 (Regulation 1612/68).

11 Regulation (EU) 492/2011 of the European Parliament and of the Council of 5 April 2011 on freedom of movement for workers within the Union, *OJ L* 2011/141, 1 (Regulation 492/2011).

prohibition, refers to the "territory of [...] Member States". Article 7(4) of these Regulations also declares any provision of collective or individual employment contracts that is in conflict with this territorially applicable prohibition of discrimination on grounds of nationality to be legally null and void.

This requirement of equal treatment as regards pay and working conditions with the workers in the State of employment was inspired not only by concern about the social protection of migrant workers, but also by the wish to protect the Member States' own workers against workers from other Member States who might be willing to work for lower social conditions. The Court of Justice for its part has linked this requirement of equal treatment with the workers of the State of employment to Article 117 EEC (now Article 152 TFEU), in which the Member States recognize the necessity to promote the workers' standard of living and working conditions. The CJEU stated expressly that the absolute nature of the prohibition of discrimination on grounds of nationality must guarantee that the nationals of the State of employment will not be harmed by any offer *to* or acceptance *by* nationals of other Member States of less favourable working conditions than those valid in the national legislation of the State of employment.[12]

However, the Court of Justice decided that a posted employee of a cross-border service provider is not a worker within the meaning of Article 39 EC (now Article 45 TFEU) and Regulation 1612/68 (now Regulation 492/1011).[13] The fact that these workers are excluded from the application of the Treaty provision on the free movement of workers has fundamental legal consequences. The question as to which employment protection scheme these workers can have recourse should, for the Court, be answered on the basis of the principles underlying the free movement of services, more specifically the right of these employees' employer to provide his services in another Member State without distinction in terms of nationality and without any other obstacles. In this legal context the application of the labour legislation of the host country has been regarded as an obstacle to the free movement of services by the employer concerned. In principle, he should have the right to continue to apply the labour law of the country of origin to his employees. In that case the possible application of the employment protection of the host State should, since it can be an obstacle to the free movement of services, be justified for reasons of public interest and be proportional to this purpose (the so-called *rule of reason*).[14]

---

12 Case 167/73, *Commission v. France*, para. 45. See also: S. Evju, "Revisiting the Posted Workers Directive: Conflict of Laws and Laws in Contrast", in: C. Barnard and O. Odudu (eds.), *The Cambridge Yearbook of European Legal Studies*, Vol. 12, 2009–2010, 153 and M. Houwerzijl, "Towards a more effective Posting Directive", in: R. Blanpain (ed.), *Freedom of Services in the European Union, Bulletin of Comparative Labour Relations*, Deventer, The Hague 2006, p. 181.

13 Cases C-49/98 et seq., *Finalarte*, paras. 22–23.

14 See, inter alia, Case C-43/93, *Vander Elst*, paras. 14 et seq.; Case C-272/94, *Guiot*, paras. 10 et seq.; Cases C-369/06 and C-374/96, *Arblade and Leloup*, paras. 33 et seq.; Cases C-49/98

With this the application of Regulation 1612/68 (now Regulation 492/1002) and of the prohibition of discrimination on grounds of nationality with regard to the pay and working conditions of Article 7 of these regulations was rendered inoperative.[15]

3.2. THE TERRITORIAL APPLICATION OF LABOUR LAW AND PRIVATE INTERNATIONAL LAW

However, the application of the principle of the prohibition of discrimination on grounds of nationality in Article 45 TFEU and in Article 7 of Regulation 492/2011 does not always guarantee cross-border workers the application of the labour legislation of the country where they work at a certain moment. In principle, the rules of private international law (PIL) remain fully applicable and on the basis of these rules it is possible that the labour legislation of another country is applicable. These rules were laid down in the Rome I Convention of 19 June 1980 (Rome I Convention).[16] At the end of 2009 this instrument was replaced by Rome I Regulation.[17]

The basis of these PIL instruments is the freedom of choice of the parties (Article 3 Rome I Convention and Article 3 Rome I Regulation). So, in principle, the parties of an employment contract have the freedom to depart from the territorial application of the labour law of the country where the activities are carried out. Still, this freedom of choice is limited. For employment contracts Articles 6 and 7 Rome I Convention and Articles 8 and 9 Rome I Regulation contain specific rules with regard to the determination of the law applicable to individual employment contracts, both in situations in which the parties have made a choice of law and in situations where no choice of law has been made. In the absence of a choice of law the principle is that the employment contract is subject to the law of the country where the employee usually carries out his job (or from where he usually carries out his job),[18] even when he is temporarily

et seq., *Finalarte*, paras. 28 et. seq.; Case C-165/98, *Mazzoleni*, paras. 22 et seq.; Case C-164/99, *Portugaia*, paras. 16 et seq.; Case C-60/03, *Wolff & Müller*, paras. 31 et seq.; Case C-346/06, *Rüffert*, para. 37; and Case C-319/06, *Commission v. Luxembourg*, paras. 42–43.

15 For a previous detailed analysis of this issue, see: H. Verschueren, "Cross-Border Workers in the European Internal Market: Trojan Horses for Member States' Labour and Social Security Law?", *International Journal of Comparative Labour Law and Industrial Relations*, 2008, 171–177.

16 Rome Convention of 19 June 1980 on the law applicable to contractual obligations, *OJ L* 1980/266, 1 (Rome I Convention).

17 Regulation (EC) 593/2008 of the European Parliament and of the Council of 17 June 2008 on the law applicable to contractual obligations (Rome I), *OJ L* 2008/177, 1 (Rome I Regulation). This regulation applies to employment contracts concluded after 17 December 2009.

18 Specifically referred to in Art. 8(2), Rome I Regulation. This was confirmed by Case C-29/10, *Koelzsch*.

employed in another country.[19] When, as a rule, this employee does not carry out his job in the same country, the law of the country where the employer's establishment is situated is applicable. However, these arrangements are put aside if the circumstances as a whole show that the employment contract is linked more closely with another country, in which case the law of that other country applies.[20] The law determined in the absence of a choice of law is sometimes referred to as "objective applicable law".

However, even if a choice of law has been made the employee may not lose the protection he enjoys on the basis of the mandatory provisions of the "objective applicable law" (Article 6(1) Rome I Convention and Article 8(1) Rome I Regulation). Moreover, pursuant to Article 7(1) Rome I Convention or Article 9 Rome I Regulation it is also possible to apply the "overriding mandatory provisions" of the law of another country. These could, for instance, be invoked if the employee is temporarily employed in that other country, as for instance in the case of posting. But the case law was and is not very clear as regards the question which "overriding mandatory provisions" can be applied to posted workers.[21]

So the application of these PIL rules, as harmonized at EU level, can have the result that work carried out on the territory of a certain Member State is not, or is only to a limited extent, subject to the labour law of that country. Indeed, according to these rules a posted employee continues to be subject to the labour legislation of the habitual place of work because he does not "habitually" work on the territory of the country in which he is temporarily posted.

3.3. THE TERRITORIAL APPLICATION OF LABOUR LAW UNDER PRESSURE AS A RESULT OF THE FREE MOVEMENT OF SERVICES

3.3.1. Free movement of services and the territorial application of labour law

However, the strict application of these PIL rules has been nuanced by the case law of the Court of Justice and, at a later stage, also by the European legislature. Indeed, the Court of Justice has not ruled out that posted employees could be made subject to a number of provisions of the labour law of the Member State in which they had been posted, provided there is a balance between the right

19 Recital 36 to the Rome I Regulation states in this regard: "As regards individual employment contracts, work carried out in another country should be regarded as temporary if the employee is expected to resume working in the country of origin after carrying out his tasks abroad."

20 See in this respect also: Case C-384/10, *Voogsgeerd* and Case C-64/12, *Schlecker*.

21 For more details on these PIL rules, see the contribution of Fieke van Overbeeke elsewhere in this book.

to free movement of services as exercised by the employers concerned and the employment protection of the employees concerned.[22]

In *Rush Portuguesa* the Court expressly stated that Union law does not prevent Member States from applying their legislation or collective labour agreements between the social partners for all those who – even temporarily – are employed on their territory, irrespective of their employer's country of establishment.[23]

The principles of the *Rush Portuguesa* judgment were once again confirmed by the Court in *Vander Elst*.[24] Still, in this judgment the Court stressed other points than in *Rush Portuguesa*. In *Vander Elst* the Court restricts itself to the national rules of public policy, such as provisions on minimum wages and starts from the idea that the application of the labour law of the country of origin, in this case Belgium, should be sufficient to exclude "any substantial risk of workers being exploited or of competition between undertakings being distorted" (paragraphs 23 and 25). In later judgments the Court stated that the application of the law of the receiving country is only allowed when the protection offered by these provisions is not offered by identical or essentially comparable obligations to which the undertaking is already held in the Member State where it is established.[25]

3.3.2. *The Posted Workers Directive*

3.3.2.1. Objectives and content

The basic principles of this case law also form the basis of the so-called Posted Workers Directive 96/71 (PWD).[26] In the first place this is apparent from the legal basis which was used for this Directive and which is part of the "free movement of services" chapter in the Treaties. There is no reference whatsoever to the Treaty provisions with regard to the free movement of workers. Its first intention is to facilitate the free movement of services by matching the Member States' legislation on the labour law applicable to posted workers.

Its provisions show that Directive 96/71 is an instrument of coordination and not of harmonization. This is explicitly confirmed by Recital 13 and in the

---

22 See, inter alia, Case C-113/89, *Rush Portuguesa*; Case C-43/93, *Vander Elst*; Case C-272/94, *Guiot*; Cases C-369/96 and C-376/96, *Arblade and Leloup*; Case C-165/98, *Mazzoleni*; Cases C-49/98 et seq., *Finalarte*; and Case C-164/99, *Portugaia*.

23 Case C-113/89, *Rush Portuguesa*, para. 18.

24 Case C-43/93, *Vander Elst*.

25 See, inter alia, Case C-445/03, *Commission v. Luxembourg*, para. 29; Case C-244/04, *Commission v. Germany*, para. 44; and Case C-168/04, *Commission v. Austria*, para. 47.

26 Directive 96/71/EC of the European Parliament and of the Council of 16 December 1996 concerning the posting of workers in the framework of the provision of services, *OJ L* 1997/18, 1 (PWD).

case law of the Court of Justice.[27] In no way does this instrument harmonizes elements of the Member States' labour law.

Therefore, this Directive can be regarded as a PIL instrument in the sense that is a particularization of Article 7 Rome I Convention and Article 9 Rome I Regulation, on the basis of which effect may be given to mandatory rules of the law of a country other than that whose law is applicable pursuant to Article 6 Rome I Convention and Article 8 Rome I Regulation.[28] This could concern the law of the country on whose territory the worker is temporarily employed. So, the PWD does not change the law applicable to the labour relations pursuant to the rules of private international law described above, but establishes, in line with what is made possible by Article 7 Rome I Convention and Article 9 Rome I Regulation, which "special" mandatory provisions of the labour law of the country of temporary employment apply, "whatever the law applicable to the employment relationship".[29] The PWD clarifies the possibility offered by PIL. It actually concerns a harmonization of what the host State could consider to be "special mandatory law" with regard to posted workers. In that sense Directive 96/71 offers the worker additional protection and strengthens the territorial scope of the labour law of the host State and the territorial application of the Member States' labour law.[30]

The Posted Workers Directive does not impose the application of all of the labour law provisions of the host State, but only of those provisions which constitute the core of the mandatory provisions for minimum protection (the so-called hard core), more specifically (see Article 3(1)): maximum work periods and minimum rest periods; minimum number of paid annual holidays; minimum wages; conditions for the posting of employees, in particular by temporary employment agencies; health, safety and hygiene in the workplace; protective measures for special groups of employees (pregnant women, youngsters); and provisions regarding equal treatment and non-discrimination.

---

27 Case C-490/04, *Commission v. Germany*, paras. 17–19; Case C-341/05, *Laval*, paras. 60, 68 and 108; and Case C-522/12, *Isbir*, para. 35.

28 See also Recital 10 of Directive 96/71. Legal doctrine also generally refers to this Directive as a special rule within the meaning of Art. 7 Rome I Convention: S. Evju, above n. 12, pp. 168–169; S. Guibboni, "Social Rights and Market Freedoms in the European Constitution: A Re-Appraisal", *ELLJ* 2010, 174; M. Houwerzijl, above n. 12, p. 184 and M. Fallon, "Le détachement européen des travailleurs à la croisée de deux logiques conflictualistes", *Rev. criv. DIP* 2008, 802–803. In the same vein see the opinion of 18 September 2014 of Advocate General Wahl in case C-396/13, *Sähköalojen ammattiliitto ry*, paras. 47–57. See more specifically on the link between the PWD and the rules of PIL: A. van Hoek and M. Houwerzijl, "'Posting' and 'Posted Workers': The Need for Clear Definitions of Two Key Concepts of the Posting of Workers Directive", in: C. Barnard and M.W. Gehring (eds.), *The Cambridge Yearbook of European Legal Studies*, Vol. 14, 2011–2012, Hart, Oxford 2012, pp. 437–443.

29 See expressly this parenthesis in Art. 3(1), first paragraph PWD.

30 S. Deakin, above n. 5, p. 594.

The Directive has laid down this hard core as part of Union law and, as a result, the Member States are obliged to apply this hard core to posted workers.[31]

However, the Directive does limit the method the Member States can use for this purpose. Only the following provisions qualify: legal and administrative provisions and/or collective agreements or arbitration awards which have been declared universally applicable and in so far as these concern the activities intended in the annex.[32] As for the collective agreements, Article 3(8) specifies which labour agreements or arbitration awards qualify, especially regarding the general validity of these norms for all undertakings that belong to the occupational group or industry concerned and are subject to the territorial scope of these agreements or decisions. Minimum wages which have not been laid down through these legal instruments are not minimum wages within the meaning of this Directive and, therefore, cannot be imposed by the Member States in the case of cross-border provision of services. The Court reached this very strict interpretation in *Laval* and *Rüffert*.[33]

The objectives of this coordination instrument are multiple, if not paradoxical.[34] Its first aim is the promotion of the free movement of services by regulating which Member State's labour law is applicable to the employees of the cross-border provider of services. Simultaneously, however, it aims at being an instrument to prevent social dumping and unfair competition. It represents a compromise between the competing interests of the Member States sending out foreign workers and those receiving them.[35] Both of these objectives have been explicitly recognized by the Court of Justice.[36] Yet the case law of the Court of Justice also makes it clear that the receiving States' room to manoeuvre with a view to applying additional elements of their labour law to posted workers is very limited. As regards the provision in Article 3(7) PWD the Court expressly stated in *Laval* that this cannot be interpreted to the effect that it allows the receiving Member State to make the performance of services dependent on compliance with terms and conditions of employment that exceed the mandatory provisions for minimum protection. The level of protection the receiving Member State has to guarantee for workers posted on its territory is, in principle, limited to the "hard core" provisions, unless, pursuant to the law or collective labour agreements valid in the Member

31 Case C-490/04, *Commission v. Germany*, para 17.

32 This concerns 13 activities, especially in construction, demolition and maintenance. On the basis of Article 3(10) the Member States can also apply collective agreements or arbitration awards to other activities.

33 Case C-341/05, *Laval*, paras. 70 and 71 and Case C-346/06, *Rüffert*, para. 31.

34 See for a recent account of this paradox, the opinion of 18 September 2014 of Advocate-General Wahl in case C-396/13, *Sähköalojen ammattiliitto ry*, paras. 26–32.

35 *Ibid.*, para. 30.

36 Case C-60/03, *Wolff & Müller*, para. 42; Case C-244/04, *Commission v. Germany*, para. 61; and Case C-341/05, *Laval*, paras. 74–75. See also the fifth recital to the PWD.

State of origin, the working conditions and circumstances are already more favourable for these workers.[37]

On the other hand, Article 3(10) PWD does allow the Member States to extend that hard core "on matters other than those [...] in the case of public policy provisions". This refers to terms and conditions of employment which are not part of the list included in Article 3(1). However, in its judgment *Commission v. Luxembourg* the Court of Justice gave a strict interpretation of these provisions. According to the Court the exception of public policy is a derogation of the fundamental principle of the free provision of services, which has to be conceived strictly and whose scope cannot be determined unilaterally by the Member States. For the Court public policy can only be invoked when there is a real and sufficiently serious threat to a fundamental interest of society.[38] This interpretation of the concept of "public policy" actually means a serious restriction of the Member States' ability to impose the application of other elements of their labour law to their posted employees on the basis of this provision.

In *Rüffert* the Court furthermore explained that the Member States, apart from their public policy claim, do not have the possibility to guarantee the avoidance of social dumping and to ensure fair competition in any other way than through the strict interpretation of the possibilities offered by the directive. In *Rüffert* the Court also expressly states that imposing minimum wages cannot be regarded as a measure to protect employees (which could possibly justify an obstacle to the free provision of services) when these wages only apply to the performance of government assignments and not to private assignments in the same industry and region.[39] Therefore the Member States can only force the employer of the posted employee to pay the minimum wages valid in the receiving Member State as laid down in the PWD. Otherwise, there would be a conflict with Article 56 TFEU, since the legislation of the host State imposes "on service providers established in another Member State where minimum rates of pay are lower an additional economic burden that may prohibit, impede or render less attractive the provision of their services in the host Member State".[40]

In the Court's opinion the strict application of the PWD and the possibilities it offers is sufficient to avoid social dumping. Thus this Directive has actually become the maximum protection which can be invoked by posted workers.[41]

---

37 Case C-341/05, *Laval*, paras. 80–81 and Case C-346/06, *Rüffert*, paras. 33–34. The Court also provides for the possibility that undertakings established in other Member States voluntarily join in a more favourable collective agreement in the receiving Member States, inter alia in the context of a commitment to their own posted workers.

38 Case C-319/06, *Commission v. Luxembourg*, paras. 29, 30, 49 and 50.

39 Case C-346/06, *Rüffert*, paras. 38–40.

40 Case C-346/06, *Rüffert*, para. 37.

41 C. Kilpatrick, "Laval's regulatory conundrum: collective standard-setting and the Court's new approach to posted workers", *European Law Review* 2009, 844–865.

The CJEU very recently confirmed this position in a judgment of 19 September 2014.[42] On the basis of his analysis of this case law, Advocate-General Wahl opines that the Court has seemingly shifted its focus from the protection of the domestic labour market to the freedom to provide services.[43] The CJEU has tried to save both objectives of the PWD. First, as an instrument of employment protection, it contributes to creating a level playing field of protection of all workers active on the territory of the host State. But, second, as an internal market instrument, it allows employers to make use of the competitive advantages of the differences in wages and employment protection between Member States.

3.3.2.2. The Member States' ability to organize efficient control of compliance with the applicable employment provisions

As Union law on the determination of the applicable labour law in the case of posting deviates from the territorial application of the labour law of the Member State where the employer concerned temporarily provides services with his own employees, efficient control of the application of these rules and of the protection offered to the employees by the PWD is of crucial importance. However, after over 15 years of application of this Directive it has now become clear that in practice there are a lot of problems as regards the legal position of posted workers. These include posting through letter-box companies, false declarations of posting, long-term postings, repeated replacements of posted workers, bogus self-employed persons,[44] non-payment of social security contributions in the sending country, non-payment of the minimum wages of the receiving country, non-observance of the rest and work periods and rules on well-being at work, failure to compensate the expenses of posting such as accommodation expenses, bad housing of the employees concerned, pyramids of sub-contractors that make control difficult, U-turn constructions through brass-plate firms, etc.[45]

---

42 Case C-549/13, *Bundesdruckerei*, para. 30.

43 Opinion in C-396/13, *Sähköalojen ammattiliitto ry*, paras. 32 et seq.

44 Compare: F. Muller, "Cross-border mobility of 'bogus' self-employed workers: a lack of legal framework coupled with protection of economic rights", *ELLJ* 2014, 306–321.

45 For recent research on these phenomena see: A. van Hoek and M. Houwerzijl, *Comparative study on the legal aspects of the posting of workers in the framework of the provision of services in het European Union*, University of Nijmegen, 2011, 363 p.; A. van Hoek and M. Houwerzijl, *Complementary study on the legal aspects of the posting of workers in the framework of the provision of services in het European Union*, University of Amsterdam, 2011, 423 p. (both of these studies available at: http://ec.europa.eu/social/main.jsp?catId=471&langId=en); N. Clark, *Regulation and Enforcement of Posted Workers Employment (POSTER), Final report*, 2012, available at: www.workinglives.org/research-themes/migrant-workers/posted-workers.cfm. See also: N. Countouris and S. Engblom, "Civilising the European Posted Workers Directive", in: M. Freedland and J. Prassl (eds.), *Viking, Laval and Beyond*, Hart, Oxford 2014, pp. 282–285 and A. van Hoek and M. Houwerzijl, above n. 28, pp. 421–437.

As regards these control measures, Article 5 PWD expressly states that the Member States have to take appropriate measures when the provisions of this directive are not complied with. In its case law the CJEU has always emphasized that the Member State whose pay and working conditions apply can enforce the application of these rules with appropriate means.[46] The CJEU accepted for instance as compatible with EU law a system of several liability of the main contractor to pay the minimum wages to his subcontractors' employees.[47] Registration prior to the employment of posted workers was also considered by the Court to be an acceptable control measure.[48] Furthermore, the Court considered the request that a translation of certain documents in the language of the receiving Member State be kept in the workplace to be justified.[49] And recently the CJEU also accepted the Belgian legislation under which the recipient of services performed by workers posted by a service provider established in another Member State is required to present the data identifying those workers to the competent authorities, before those workers begin to work.[50]

However, control measures in the receiving State can run into legal limits. According to the Court these measures are also subject to a *rule of reason* test.[51] A number of national control measures failed this test, such as the obligation to draft and retain social documents in accordance with the legislation of the host State while the service provider concerned already had to keep similar records pursuant to the legislation of the Member State where he was established.[52] The Court also criticized the fact that prior to the posting permission had to be asked for the employment and entry of posted workers who are not nationals of a Member State.[53] More recently the Court ruled that, with regard to the self-employed, the information requested by Belgium prior to the beginning of the activities was too detailed.[54] The Court, however, expressly confirmed in this judgment that the objective of combating social fraud and prevention of abuse, notably false self-employment and moonlighting, can be objectives to justify possible restrictions of the free movement of services. In this respect the Court also referred to the objective of protecting the financial balance of the social

46 Case C-62–63/81, *Seco*, para. 14; Case C-113/89, *Rush Portuguesa*, para. 18; Cases C-369/06 and C-374/96, *Arblade en Leloup*, paras. 38, 61–63 and 74; Case C-168/04, *Commission v. Austria*, para. 47; and Case C-244/04, *Commission v. Germany*, para. 36.

47 Case C-60/03, *Wolff & Müller*.

48 This possibility was expressly recognized by the Court of Justice in Case C-244/04, *Commission v. Germany*, para. 41.

49 Case C-490/04, *Commission v. Germany*, paras. 71–72.

50 Case C-315/13, *De Clercq*.

51 See specifically Cases C-369/06 and C-374/96, *Arblade and Leloup*, paras. 36. See also Case C-60/03, *Wolff & Müller*, paras. 28–30; Case C-445/03, *Commission v. Luxembourg*, para. 40; and Case C-244/04, *Commission v. Germany*, para. 36.

52 Cases C-369/06 and C-374/96, *Arblade and Leloup*.

53 Case C-168/04, *Commission v. Austria* and Case C-91/13, *Essent Energie Products*.

54 Case C-577/10, *Commission v. Belgium*, para. 55.

security schemes, the objective of preventing unfair competition and social dumping and the objective of protecting employees and self-employed persons.[55]

As a result of this restrictive case law of the Court of Justice in the context of the increasing use, according to some misuse, of posting in the EU internal market, the demand for more mandatory European rules on the enforcement of the provisions of the PWD has been getting louder and louder. In this context Directive 2014/67/EU was adopted on 15 May 2014.[56] This new Enforcement Directive is intended to establish a general framework of measures and control mechanisms that should lead to a better and more uniform implementation, application and enforcement of the PWD in practice, including measures to prevent and fight any misuse and skirting of the applicable rules. For instance, in this new Directive an indicative, non-exhaustive list of qualitative criteria has been included which relate to the temporary nature inherent to the concept of posting as well as to the existence of a real link between the employer and the Member State from where the posting takes place (Article 4). Its intention is to prevent all forms of misuse, for instance long-term postings, repeated replacements of posted workers or the use of so-called letter-box firms. If such misuses are identified, the PWD would not be applicable. However, this new Directive does not indicate which employment law would then be applicable to the workers concerned. Presumably this would be the law of the host State.

A crucial provision in the new Directive is Article 9. This article outlines which control measures may be taken by the receiving Member State. It has been agreed that this list will not be limitative. However, in exchange the European Commission was given the mandate to test all other measures the Member States could take against the requirements set by the Court of Justice with regard to the prohibition of obstructing the free movement of services in a disproportionate way.

Article 12 contains another important provision, more specifically several liability in the case of sub-contracting. The Member States can introduce forms of several liability of the direct main contractor. As for the construction industry, this is said to amount to an obligation. Furthermore, the Member States can also apply several liability to contracts of other intermediaries than the direct contracting parties.

We will have to wait and see whether this Enforcement Directive is an efficient instrument to counter the misuse in posting. Still, it is a fact that this Directive does not change the legal framework within which posting is possible, nor the employment protection for the posted workers. The regulatory

---

55 Case C-577/10, *Commission v. Belgium*, para. 45.

56 Directive 2014/67/EU of the European Parliament and of the Council of 15 May 2014 on the enforcement of Directive 96/71/EC concerning the posting of workers in the framework of the provision of services and amending Regulation (EU) No 1024/2012 on administrative cooperation through the Internal Market Information System ("the IMI Regulation"), *OJ L* 2014/159, 11 (Enforcement Directive).

competition within a Member State made possible by this continues to be maintained.

3.4. THE POSTED WORKERS' POSITION AT THE CROSSROADS OF LEGAL RULES AND OF ECONOMIC INTERESTS

From the previous analysis it follows that pursuant to Union law the posted workers' position in terms of labour law is situated at the intersection of applicable rules of law. In addition, it is also at the crossroads of the economic interests of the parties concerned, i.e. the Member States, the employees and the employers (both those making use of posting and those normally economically active in the receiving country).

As far as the rules of law are concerned, this is a matter of the territorial application of labour law and the principle of equal treatment for all work carried out on the territory of a Member State on the one hand, and the "country of origin principle" of free movement of services on the other. Both are guaranteed by Union law. The first principle aims not only at protecting cross-border workers by giving them the right to the same treatment as the other workers in the State of employment, but also at protecting the latter against social competition by the migrant workers. The second principle aims at protecting the cross-border service providers against unjustified obstacles to the free movement of services that would be used if the country where the party concerned temporarily provides services were to try to apply its own rules of law to that party. It illustrates the "trade-off between regulatory neutrality and regulatory competition [which] accounts for fundamental ambiguity of internal market law towards social dumping".[57]

The PWD and the strict interpretation by the CJEU of the possibilities the receiving States have with a view to granting supplementary protection to the posted employee, on top of the protection offered by this Directive, strike a legally precarious balance between those two principles. This precariousness is even reinforced by the critical attitude of the CJEU with regard to the control measures used by the receiving Member States to assert the right application of the rules of law concerned. The recent discussion within the Council of Ministers about the Enforcement Directive proposed by the European Commission is a perfect illustration of this.

[57] A. Saydé, "One Law, Two Competitions: An Enquiry into the Contradictions of Free Movement Law", in: C. Barnard and O. Odudu (eds.), *Cambridge Yearbook of Legal Studies*, Vol. 13, 2010–2011, Hart, Oxford 2012, p. 408; and A. Saydé, *Abuse of EU Law and the Regulation of the Internal Market*, Hart, Oxford 2014, pp. 309–314.

This discrepancy was especially striking in *Vicoplus*.[58] In this case the Court of Justice held that workers posted by a temporary employment agency actually do enter the labour market of the Member State to which they are posted and therefore do fall within the transitional provisions on the free movement of workers in the Accession Treaties. The Court holds the view that these workers effectively enter the labour market of the host Member State because during the period of their posting the posted workers normally have a job within the user undertaking which would have otherwise have been carried out by workers of that undertaking.[59]

However, the Court does not conclude that these workers are migrating workers within the meaning of Article 45 TFEU, for in that case they could invoke the right to equal treatment with the local workers. But the judgment does indicate that the posting is at the crossroads of two elements of Union law on the internal market, notably the free movement of workers and the free movement of services. With regard to the employment protection of these workers the Court continues to give priority to the provisions on the free movement of services.[60]

In the Council of Europe too there was criticism of the approach in the PWD and the case law of the Court of Justice. As a result of a collective complaint against Sweden the European Committee of Social Rights in a decision of 3 July 2013 was very critical of the restrictions imposed by the PWD and the case law of the Court of Justice regarding the application of Swedish labour law to workers posted in Sweden.[61] Formally the complaint was against the Swedish legislation which had transposed the CJEU's case law into national law, especially in the aforementioned cases *Laval, Rüffert* and *Commission v. Luxembourg*. In the context of this contribution it is particularly important to note the Committee's view that the Swedish legislation is in conflict with Article 19(4) of the European Social Charter which orders the States not to treat foreign workers less favourably than their own workers as regards wages, working conditions and collective bargaining. The Committee does recognize that posted workers find themselves in a special situation and that they differ from migrant workers who go and work for an employer in another Member State on their own initiative. But for the Committee posted workers are workers who reside and work legally on the territory of the host country. Therefore they fall within the application

58 Cases C-307/09 et seq., *Vicoplus et al.*

59 Cases C-307/09 et seq., *Vicoplus et al.*, paras. 31–32.

60 The Court took the same ambiguous position in Cases C-611/10 and C-612/10, *Hudzinski* and *Wawrzyniak*. In this judgment the Court held the view that posted workers could invoke the Treaty provisions on the free movement of workers (Articles 45–48 TFEU) to receive social benefits (in this case family benefits) from the host State.

61 European Committee of Social Rights, Decision of 3 July 2013, complaint no. 85/2012, *Swedish Union Confederation (LO) and Swedish Confederation of Professional Employees (TCO) v. Sweden*. See also on the decision: M. Rocca, "A clash of kings. The European Committee of Social Rights on the 'Lex Laval' … and on the EU framework for the posting of workers", *European Journal of Social Law* 2014, 217–232.

of the prohibition of discrimination of Article 19(4) of the Social Charter. So, for the Committee, during their stay and employment they have the right to equal treatment with the host country's own workers as regards pay and other employment terms.[62] Furthermore, the Committee holds the view that the restrictions on collective actions, which pursuant to the Swedish legislation are only allowed if their purpose is to guarantee a minimum protection for the posted workers, and not if their purpose is to effectively obtain the same employment protection as the country's own workers, are in conflict with Article 19(4)(b) and Article 6 (the right to collective bargaining and collective action) of the European Social Charter.

In this decision the Committee makes no attempt to disguise its criticism of the legal order of the EU. It does recognize that facilitating cross-border service provision by the posting employer is an important part of the economic freedoms of the EU, which are held in high esteem by the Committee. But from the perspective of the values, principles and fundamental rights laid down in the European Social Charter these market freedoms cannot *a priori* be more valuable than these fundamental rights. For the Committee Union law must be interpreted and applied to the effect that, among other things, it must recognize the fundamental right to equal treatment and the fundamental right of trade unions to strive for the protection and improvement of the living and working conditions of the employees.[63]

Besides, posting is not only to be found at the crossroads of the free movement of workers and the right to equal treatment on the one hand and the free movement of services of the employer on the other; legally it is also situated on the crossroads of Union law on the free movement of workers and Union law concerning the rules applicable to an employment contract (PIL). Pursuant to the rules in the Rome I Convention and Rome I Regulation, the law of the country of habitual employment applies to the employment contract, and this country is not supposed to change in the case of temporary employment in another country, among which posting activities.[64] However, the theoretical continuation of the application of the law of the country of habitual employment can be mitigated by the application of "overriding mandatory provisions" or rules of "public policy (*ordre public*)" of another country, in particular the country where a posted worker temporarily works. The source of inspiration of the PIL rules is the protection of the weaker contracting party.[65] In this respect too the PWD tried to find a balance. But although the applicable PIL rules give

62 See paras. 134, 136, 140 and 141 of the Decision.

63 See paras. 121 and 122 of the Decision.

64 Note that the "country of habitual employment" in the PIL rules is not necessarily the same as the "country of origin" of the employers within the meaning of EU internal market law. See on this issue: A. van Hoek and M. Houwerzijl, above n. 28, pp. 440–442.

65 See in this vein the use by the Court of Justice of the concept of "*favor laboratoris*" in the application of the Rome I Convention in Case C-29/10, *Koelzsch*, para. 46.

the receiving Member State a certain level of flexibility to apply parts of its employment protection, the Court of Justice in its case law on the PWD has seriously restricted this flexibility by stating that these Member States may not impose protection that exceeds the protection allowed by the PWD. Otherwise there would be a conflict with EU internal market law.

From the fact that in its case law the Court interprets any abrogation of the country of origin principle very strictly, it is clear that the Court implicitly gives priority to the interests of those that make use of the free movement of services.[66] In so doing the Court has paved the way for the use of the competitive advantage offered by the possibility to carry out activities and provide services in a Member State under employment conditions which apply in another (read cheaper) Member State, with the exception of the "hard core" provisions listed in Article 3(1) PWD. This was even recognized by the European Commission in a recent document in which it states that "posting workers allows companies to exploit their competitive advantages across borders".[67]

According to some authors,the CJEU's case law distorted the "the delicate balance between competing objectives".[68] This case law is also said to run counter to what the authors of the Directive intended in 1996. It is said to have offered more room for manoeuvre to the receiving Member States through the provisions of Article 3(7) and (10) PWD.[69] In any case, as a result the regulatory competition regarding wage and employee protection between the Member States is being imported into the Member States themselves.[70] Moreover, it overturns the principle of territorial application of the labour law of the Member States which was laid down in the EEC Treaty of 1957, more specifically in the instruments regarding the freedom of movement for workers, thus allowing the exploitation of the competitive advantage of companies established in Member States with low wage standards.[71]

The discussion on this regulatory competition within the territory of a Member State differs from the discussion on the regulatory competition

66 See in the same vein: C. Barnard, above n. 4, pp. 226–227; S. Deakin, above n. 5, pp. 596–597 and S. Evju, above n. 12, p. 154.

67 European Commission, *Employment and Social Developments in Europe 2014,* December 2014, 154.

68 N. Countouris and S. Engblom, above n. 45, p. 282.

69 See M. Biagi, "Fortune smiles on the Italian EU Presidency: talking half-seriously about the posted workers and parental leave directives", *International Journal of Comparative Labour Law and Industrial Relations* 1996, 104; M. Biagi, "The 'posted workers' EU directive: from social dumping to social protectionism", in: R. Blanpain (ed.), *Labour Law and Industrial Relations. Bulletin of Comparative Labour Relations*, Kluwer, The Hague 1997, pp. 177–178; and C. Kilpatrick, "Internal market architecture and the accommodation of labour rights", in: Ph. Syrpis (ed.), *The Judiciary, the Legislature and the EU Internal Market,* Cambridge University Press, Cambridge 2012, pp. 212–213 and 222–223.

70 S. Deakin, above n. 5, p. 597 and N. Countouris and S. Engblom, above n. 45, pp. 285–286.

71 S. Guibboni, "European citizenship, labour law and social rights in times of crisis", *European Journal of Social Law* 2013, 203–204.

between Member States. In the latter case this concerns goods and services produced in a Member State through cheap labour and subsequently exported to another Member State. Differences in standards of living and productivity could perhaps be a justification for this regulatory competition between Member States. Very recently the Court of Justice explicitly acknowledged that such regulatory competition is fully lawful in the context of the EU internal market. Member States to which goods or services produced in another Member State are exported may not require that for the production of such goods or services the minimum wages fixed by their legislation should apply. The Court said that by imposing a minimum wage linked to the cost of living in that Member State, but without relation to the cost of living in the Member State in which the services are performed, the first Member State prevents subcontractors established in this Member State from deriving a competitive advantage from the differences between the respective rates of pay. For the Court, this goes beyond what is necessary to ensure that the objective of employee protection is attained.[72] However, this labour cost competition is far less justifiable if the wage competition occurs on the territory of one and the same Member State. In that case one can hardly refer to a difference in labour costs justified by the difference in productivity and standard of living.

Nonetheless, for others a Member State's wish to apply its own pay and employment protection to posted workers is inspired by protectionist motives, more specifically with a view to shielding its own undertakings from competition within the European internal market, said to be practised by undertakings from other Member States.[73] Furthermore, the application of the labour law of the host country to (potentially) posted workers from another Member State is not always considered to be in the interests of the posted workers themselves. It could also be the case that as a result of the application of the receiving State's labour law, posting in that country is no longer profitable for the principal, with the effect that the secondment does not take place and the employee concerned runs the risk of losing his job. From this point of view wage competition is not regarded as unfair competition, but rather as a normal form of competition within the European internal market and "the natural functioning of economic integration".[74] Even the PWD itself would have unacceptable protective characteristics, like being "anti-competitive" and "socially problematic", since it would protect local workers and would prevent workers from other countries

72 Judgment of 18 September 2014 in Case C- 549/13, *Bundesdruckerei*, para. 34.

73 See, inter alia, R. Giesen, "Posting: social protection of workers vs. fundamental freedoms?", *CMLRev.* 2003, 145–147 and 156–158 and D. Kukovec, "Law and the Periphery", *ELJ* 2015, 406–408. See also the position taken by some parties in cases before the Court of Justice as reflected in the opinions of the Advocates General in Case C-49/98 et seq., *Finalarte*, paras. 32–33, Case C-164/00, *Portugaia*, para. 15 and Case C-445/03, *Commission v. Luxembourg*, para. 51.

74 A. Saydé, *Abuse of EU Law and the Regulation of the Internal Market*, above n. 57, p. 314.

from "exploiting their lower wages as a competitive advantage in the internal market".[75]

4. CONCLUSION

The European internal market has unmistakably fuelled and strengthened social competition between the workers of the Member States. It offers undertakings and employers the possibility of skirting the labour legislation applicable in the Member State in which the employee actually works, or to avoid its application altogether. This is especially the case for employees in cross-border employment. At the time of the establishment of the PWD in the 1990s,[76] as well as very recently during the discussions in the Council of Ministers about the proposal for the Enforcement Directive, it was obvious that the traditional posting States, i.e. States with high unemployment figures and low levels of social protection, want to offer their undertakings as many opportunities as possible to use their competitive advantage on the European internal market through the cross-border posting of workers. The application of the labour law of the host country is only guaranteed to a limited extent, as a result of which this Member State is faced with internal social competition.

More than ever before, the European Union with its internal market continues to struggle with the balance between, on the one hand, the freedoms of the internal market and, on the other, the social protection the separate Member States have introduced. From the above it is clear that the PWD and the case law of the Court of Justice try to reconcile, with disputable success, prevention of unfair competition on the one hand and the guarantee of effective competition on the other.[77]

For some authors, the answer to this is more European social regulation, inter alia by using framework directives that would leave room to manoeuvre for the national legislature. Fundamental social rights should also play a bigger part in this debate. The fields where labour law has been harmonized so far are too limited and offer no solution for the social competition that has arisen within the European internal market.[78] Others in their turn advocate a cutting back of the

---

75 F. Mustili and J. Pelkmans, *Access Barriers to Services Markets. Mapping, tracing, understanding and measuring*, CEPS Special Report No. 77/2013, Brussels, 2013, 51.

76 See inter alia: M. Biagi, "Fortune smiles on the Italian EU Presidency: talking half-seriously about the posted workers and parental leave directives", above n. 69, pp. 97–109 and S. Evju, above n. 12, pp. 165–174.

77 M. Biagi, "The 'posted workers' EU directive: from social dumping to social protectionism", above n. 69, pp. 178–180 and M. Fallon, above n. 28, pp. 811–812 and 817–818.

78 See, inter alia, N. Countouris and S. Engblom, above n. 45, pp. 290–292; S. Guibboni, "European citizenship, labour law and social rights in times of crisis", *European Journal of Social Law* 2013, 194–216; and S. Klosse, "Balancing Europe's Economic and Social Goals: Fighting a Losing Battle?', *European Journal of Social Law* 2012, 176–192.

European internal market's influence on national labour law and, in particular, on its territorial application. Labour law should in the first place remain the responsibility and competence of the Member States.[79] In this context some propose the introduction in the PWD of more possibilities for the host State to apply parts of its employment protection to posted workers, possibly through Article 3(7) PWD.[80]

As for the first option, it remains unclear to what extent more European labour legislation will lead to more and better employment protection. However, recent discussions on the proposals of the Commission, for instance on the Enforcement Directive, have in shown that it is very difficult to achieve a political agreement at the European level in this respect. The risk that the European labour legislation which would come about in this context would rather lead to a decrease in the social protection of workers is not unreal.

As for the second option, the European institutions, among which the Court of Justice, will indeed have to be prepared to limit the influence of the so-called negative market integration on national social law by giving the Member States more room to manoeuvre with regard to the social legislation they want to apply.

79 See for instance: C. Joerges and F. Rödl, "Informal Politics, Formalised Law and the 'Social Deficit' of European Integration: Reflections after the Judgments of the ECJ in *Viking* and *Laval*", *ELJ* 2009, 1–19.

80 N. Countouris and S. Engblom, above n. 45, pp. 287–288.

CHAPTER 5
THE TENSE RELATIONSHIP BETWEEN LABOUR MARKET RIGHTS AND RESPECT FOR DIGNITY AT WORK: EUROPEAN DIMENSION

Barbara KRESAL*

1. LABOUR MARKET AS AN INTEGRAL PART OF A BROADER CONCEPT OF THE MARKET

The Treaty on the Functioning of the European Union (TFEU)[1] defines the internal market in Article 26 as "an area without internal frontiers in which the free movement of kgoods, persons, services and capital is ensured". These four fundamental freedoms form one of the cornerstones of the EU and constitute the basis of the internal market.

The labour market, which is one of the aspects of the free movement of persons within the EU, is thus framed in the broader concept of the internal market. The labour market in general, as well as labour market rights, cannot be separated from other markets that have been established and promoted in current capitalist society. So the labour market is an integral part of a broader concept of the market. This concept is understood as the "selling and buying of commodities". There are goods and services markets, a capital market, different submarkets and supramarkets, etc. We are living in a (perhaps social) market economy.[2] Actually, the entire society is transforming into a

* Professor of Labour Law and Social Security, University of Ljubljana.

1 OJ C 326, 26.10.2012, pp. 47–390 (consolidated version).

2 Article 3 of the Treaty on European Union (TEU) (OJ C 326, 26.10.2012, pp. 13–390 – consolidated version) states that the internal market shall work for the sustainable development of the EU which shall be based, among other things, on a highly competitive social market economy. Full employment and social progress are mentioned in connection with this notion, and in the same provision reference is also made to social justice, equality and solidarity, to mention just a few. However, it seems that these general goals, objectives of the EU and the aims of the internal market are often overlooked when designing the policies and measures within the EU or when evaluating these policies and measures or when judging

market society.[3] Under the pressure of economic (neo)liberalism, everything is gradually becoming a commodity (or, to be more exact, everything is treated as if it were a commodity). This process is often described as a commodification.

When speaking about the labour market(s) within the EU, one has to ask the question whether a single EU labour market really exists. The relationship between the national/regional/local labour markets and the EU labour market, as well as the relationship between these labour markets and the global labour market, is very important and must not be neglected. They interfere with each other, overlap each other and compete against each other.

Another introductory remark has to be made in relation to the terminology that is used in connection with the notion "labour market". Usually, a distinction is made between the "free" labour market, the "regulated" labour market and the "rigid" labour market. The "rigid" labour market is supposed to be the one that is "over-regulated". However, it has to be emphasized that the terminology is never value-free. All types of labour markets are regulated[4] and it is not true that a "free" labour market is less regulated. There are a lot of strict rules with very efficient sanctions protecting the "free" labour market. However, it is regulated according to the values of the "free market economy", following (neo)liberal economic principles.

One of the neoliberal dogmas is that the market in itself is kind of a natural state of art, which needs no rules for its functioning and, consequently, every regulation of the market represents an obstacle, a barrier to the "natural" rules of the market. However, the "free" market is not without rules; on the contrary, it has to be highly regulated in order to function according to the values of the (neo)liberal model. Thus, only particular rules and regulations which do not fit into the neoliberal model are considered as over-regulation (rigid), whereas rules and regulations which do fit into the neoliberal model are considered as a natural state of art, and are therefore not perceived as over-regulation.

So when saying that the labour market has to be "liberalized", i.e. that "obstacles" and "barriers" (meaning labour regulations, safety regulations etcetera) have to be removed in order to achieve a "free" labour market,[5] we

---

them, etc. It seems that the *social* market economy of the EU has not yet learned how to be social.

3 Rigaux points out that "under the impulse of the EU more and more systems are getting subject to market laws" and that "the society has been replaced by the market" (M. Rigaux, "Labour Law or Social Competition Law? The right to dignity of working people questioned (once again)", in: M. Rigaux, J. Buelens and A. Latinne (eds.), *From Labour Law to Social Competition Law?*, Intersentia, Cambridge/Antwerp/Portland 2014, p. 7).

4 A market is only (perceived as) over-regulated if there are rules which do not correspond to the values of a particular system/ideology according to which the evaluation is made. Only such rules are (perceived as) rigid.

5 "Liberalization" and "freedom" are words with very positive connotations, whereas the words "obstacle" and "barrier" have a negative connotation. It is not a coincidence that the words "liberalization" and "freedom" are used for the kind of labour market that follows the rules of

have to bear in mind that this is (neo)liberal terminology. The same situation could also be described as a situation in which someone would like to (over-)regulate the relationship between capital and labour, with rules that follow the values of the neoliberal ideology. It does not matter how many of such rules are needed; it does not matter if such rules represent obstacles and barriers to the workers in terms of achieving decent remuneration, better working conditions, full employment, etc.

2. (NEO)LIBERAL MODEL AND THE PRECARISATION OF SOCIETY

In the neoliberal model, workers are treated as if they were a commodity[6] on the "free" labour market (it is overlooked that they are persons with human rights) and labour law is perceived as a system of rigid rules, as costs and as an obstacle to the "free" labour market. National labour laws are compared on the basis of labour costs analyses. That leads to "law shopping", a phenomenon in which countries, too, are treated as if they were a commodity on the global market of legislative products.[7] Law shopping results in social dumping where countries try to gain a competitive advantage by carrying out labour law reforms aimed at lowering labour costs, i.e. lowering labour protection, wages, workers' rights. Countries are under a lot of pressure, which is measured by different indexes and a ranking according to which countries have less "rigid" labour laws and lower labour costs. The result is a deregulation process. This process has been going on for some time now. It is a "race to the bottom". All of the above leads to worse working conditions, precarious work and consequently, to a precarious life for numerous people and, finally, to precarious societies in general. In such a model, the right to dignity at work is not respected and the rights of working people to decent working conditions and decent wages are threatened.

This pressure of the neoliberal ideology has become stronger, especially since the 1980s. It has become even stronger during the recent crisis. In the field of labour relations, the neoliberal ideology is characterized by the promotion of different forms of non-standard work with less labour and social protection, by the contractualization of labour, due to which more and more people

the neoliberal model, whereas the words "obstacles" and "barriers" are used for the rules that the neoliberal model would like to erase.

6 See B. Kresal, "Mutating or dissolving labour law? The fundamental right to dignity of working people questioned (once again)", in: M. Rigaux, J. Buelens and A. Latinne (eds.), *From Labour Law to Social Competition Law?*, Intersentia, Cambridge/Antwerp/Portland 2014, pp. 149, 152–153.

7 See A. Supiot, *L'esprit de Philadelphie: la justice sociale face au marché total*, Seuil, Paris 2010, pp. 65–67, 80; M. Rigaux, above n. 3, pp. 7, 10–11 and others.

are working outside the scope of full labour law protection (outsourcing, subcontracting, (false) self-employment, (false) posting of workers, etc.), by non-observance of workers' rights in practice, by the introduction of general labour law reforms with less protection for the workers, and by the transformation of the collective bargaining system towards decentralization and the conclusion of less favourable collective agreements.

All of this is going on in the name of lower labour costs and higher competitiveness. It is supposed to boost growth and create new jobs and resolve the problems of the crisis. Unsurprisingly, this is not happening.[8] What it is doing, however, is causing segmentation of the labour markets, making employment more precarious, increasing people's inequality, dependency and insecurity, and resulting in a higher risk of people being denied the right to work, decent wages and decent working and living conditions in general.

3. THE EUROPEAN UNION IS FOLLOWING THE SAME NEOLIBERAL TRENDS

These neoliberal trends described in the previous chapters can also be seen within the European context. Many examples of this can be found.

For instance, the development of EU directives in the field of labour law shows how the role, the strength and the actual or desired potential of labour law have been changing over time. In short, the EU's legislative activity in the field of labour law from the origins of the European integration in the 1950s up until now can be described as: late start (in the 1970s), development (1970s and part of the 1980s), stagnation (from the 1990s on), degradation (in recent years, especially since the recent crisis).

Today, we cannot see any strength in the EU's legislative power when it comes to labour law. Nevertheless, today the EU has a strong(er) influence over national labour laws than ever before in the history of the European integration process. However, this influence is non-transparent and lacks a foundation in democratic decision-making. It does not take place within the law-making competences of the EU in the field of labour law. It rather comes from the country-specific recommendations (CSRs) and the memorandums of understanding (MoUs).

MoUs are perhaps the most extreme example. The countries that entered the so-called economic adjustment programme and signed the MoU (Greece, Ireland, Portugal, etc.) were bound by a bilateral agreement with the European

8 See how the EU's policy during the crisis and its austerity trap was described by Raymond Torres when publishing the ILO World of Work Report in 2012: "The prescribed cure is killing the patient". International Labour Organization (International Institute for Labour Studies), *World of work report 2012: Better jobs for a better economy* (ed. R. Torres), ILO, Geneva 2012; press release 30 April 2012, available at: http://ilo.org/global/research/global-reports/world-of-work/WCMS_179857/lang--en/index.htm.

Commission, the European Central Bank and the International Monetary Fund, i.e. the "Troika"; within this framework different measures were imposed upon these countries as a condition for financial aid.[9] Those measures included vast structural reforms in the field of labour law, social security and other fields with the aim of lowering labour costs, making the social security system less expensive and making the country more "competitive" and attractive for business.

Some of these measures were found to be contrary to the European and/or international binding legal instruments on fundamental labour rights and minimum labour standards (see, for example, the decisions of the ILO's Committee on Freedom of Association referring to the ILO Conventions Nos 87 and 98 or the conclusions of the European Committee of Social Rights referring to the Council of Europe's European Social Charter).[10] Although the EU does not have any legislative power concerning wages or the social partners' freedom of association, the Troika interfered with the countries' minimum wage regulation, collective bargaining system, etc. This influence of the EU (indirect, nevertheless very strong influence via the Troika) upon national labour laws lacks transparency as well as democratic legitimacy.

Although the CSRs are not formally binding instruments (they are "recommendations"), they exert strong pressure on the Member States since they do have potential financial and other negative consequences in the event of non-observance. Within the framework of this system of economic governance and coordination of national policies, which results in a list of recommendations based on the periodical reviews of the economic and social performance of the countries, numerous structural reforms in the field of labour law and social security have been implemented in different EU Member States in recent years. Many recommendations are directed towards a more "flexible", "free" labour market and they fit well into the neoliberal agenda.

Another example of the neoliberal approach within the EU is the so-called REFIT Programme, the new Regulatory Fitness and Performance Programme. Once again, the neoliberal ideology is reflected in the terminology. The aim of this programme of the European Commission is to "make EU law simpler and to reduce regulatory costs",[11] including in the field of labour law. Legal rules

---

9 See, for example, M.-C. Escande-Varniol, S. Laulom, E. Mazuyer and P. Vielle (eds.), *Quel droit social dans une Europe en crise?*, Larcier, Brussels 2012 and many others.

10 For more see, for example, N. Bruun, K. Lörcher and I. Schömann (eds.), *The Economic and Financial Crisis and Collective Labour Law in Europe*, Hart Publishing, Oxford/Portland 2014, especially the contributions by N. Bruun, "Legal and Judicial International Avenues: The ILO" (pp. 243–264), K. Lörcher, "Legal and Judicial Avenues: The (Revised) European Social Charter" (pp. 265–194), and K. Ewing and J. Hendy QC, "International Litigation Possibilities in Collective Labour Law: ECHR" (pp. 295–321).

11 See the European Commission's internet page titled "Smart Regulation", available at: http://ec.europa.eu/smart-regulation/refit/index_en.htm. See also European Commission, Regulatory Fitness and Performance Programme (REFIT): State of Play and Outlook (SWD

are subject to the nowadays mainstream conventions constructed by the media, the fashion industry and other interested stakeholders: they have to be fit and slim. How is it possible to make (labour) legislation fitter and slimmer? Shall we send legal rules to the fitness centre? Legal rules are no athletes, movie stars or models; legal rules should be the expression of the sovereignty of people, taking into account the interests of all groups and individuals, and based on transparent and democratic processes.

The entire response of the EU to the recent financial and economic crisis has been led by neoliberal principles. MoUs, CSRs and the REFIT programme are just a few examples of that.

The current negotiations on the TTIP agreement fit well into this neoliberal EU policy too. The Transatlantic Trade and Investment Partnership between the EU and the United States has been negotiated in secrecy. Although the negotiations started in July 2013, the EU position paper "Directives for the negotiation on the Transatlantic Trade and Investment Partnership between the European Union and the United States of America" from 17 June 2013 was classified as a restricted document for more than a year and was only made public in October 2014,[12] after strong pressure and demands from civil society. Since then, the European Commission has made great efforts to prove that the process is transparent.

There are many studies that show the potential negative impact of the TTIP[13] on labour and social rights, as well as on other important areas, such as environmental protection, health and safety of products, chemicals, restriction of GMOs (genetically modified organisms), consumer protection, etc.

One of the main goals of the TTIP is to remove non-tariff, regulative "barriers", i.e. the legal rules that generate costs for businesses.[14] The TTIP could

(2014) 192 final, Brussels, 18.06.2014, COM (2014) 368 final, available at: http://ec.europa.eu/smart-regulation/docs/com2014_368_en.pdf.

12 European Union, Declassification of the document ST 11103/13 restreint UE/EU restricted, 17.06.2013, "Directives for the negotiation on the Transatlantic Trade and Investment Partnership between the European Union and the United States of America", Council of the European Union, Brussels, 9 October 2014; new status of the document: public, available at: http://data.consilium.europa.eu/doc/document/ST-11103-2013-DCL-1/en/pdf.

13 See, for example, W. Raza et al., *Assessing the Claimed Benefits of the Transatlantic Trade and Investment partnership (TTIP)*, OFSE – Austrian Foundation for Development Research, Vienna 2014; M. Myant, "The Transatlantic Trade and Investment partnership: exaggerated hopes from the liberalising agenda?", ETUI Policy Brief, No 4/2014, ETUI, Brussels 2014; and other studies. Compare to the European Commission's assessment, for example, see European Commission, Impact Assessment Report on the future of the EU-US trade relations, Strasbourg, 12.03.2013, SWD(2013) 68 final, available at: http://trade.ec.europa.eu/doclib/docs/2013/march/tradoc_150759.pdf, and European Commission, Transatlantic Trade and Investment Partnership: The Economic Analysis Explained, September 2013, available at: http://trade.ec.europa.eu/doclib/docs/2013/september/tradoc_151787.pdf.

14 The position paper, for example, says that the TTIP shall "provide for the highest possible level of legal protection and certainty for investors", whereas when dealing with labour and social rights and other protective legal regulations, the TTIP recognizes the right of the EU

also threaten the public sector, for example in education and other important areas, promote privatization of the public sector and, the most delicate and discussed issue, it is supposed to regulate the ISDS (investor-state dispute settlement) mechanism which is seen as one of the greatest threats posed by the TTIP. If the ISDS mechanism were to be included in the TTIP, investors would have the right to sue countries through international arbitration, challenging countries' legal regulations or a particular measure, for example, raising the minimum wage level, if they consider that country's protective measure to be unjustified and to interfere with their interests. However, no similar legal possibility is provided in the TTIP to ensure the protection of the public interest, workers' rights, the environment, etc. against investors' actions.[15]

The TTIP negotiations are often presented as a way of reconciling the conflicting interests of (social) Europe and the (liberal) US; the question whether the EU will be able to preserve its "European social model" is often posed as a crucial one. However, the TTIP is just one of many attempts to strengthen the neoliberal rules all over the globalized world and it pursues the common (and not conflicting) interests of business on both sides of the Atlantic and fits very well into the current neoliberal EU policy as well. Therefore, the TTIP sharpens the conflict of interests between capital, mainly represented by multinational corporations from the US and the EU, trying to increase profits, on one side, and on the other side, workers, consumers, the majority of ordinary people on both sides of the Atlantic and in other parts of the world who are pushed into the irrational precarization of society, who are pushed into social dumping and who are burdened by the risk that respect for human dignity will be neglected.

The development of the case law of the European Court of Justice also reflects the strengthening of the neoliberal approach within the EU. Whereas in early years, and especially in the 1970s, the Court often promoted the social aspect of European integration, recent case law strengthens the economic freedoms at the expense of the social aspect of the Union. Recently, the free labour market rights have been frequently reinforced by the CJEU.

---

and countries to regulate these matters. However, this right is limited to "measures necessary to pursue legitimate public policy objectives such as social, environmental, security". So, the TTIP, if concluded, would ensure the highest possible protection for investors, businesses, and it would allow/tolerate only the necessary (i.e. minimum, as "fit and slim" as possible) protection for workers, consumers, etc. All other types of regulation in these fields would be considered as obstacles or barriers which would have to be removed.

15 The position paper explicitly states that "the agreement will include mechanisms to support the promotion of decent work through effective domestic implementation of ILO core labour standards". Why are only the core labour standards promoted and why only through domestic mechanisms? Why are domestic courts and dispute settlement mechanisms not sufficient for investors too? For more on the ISDS see, for example, ILO, *Social dimension of free trade agreements*, Geneva 2013.

Well-known cases such as *Laval un Partneri*,[16] *Rüffert*[17] and *Commission v. Luxembourg*[18] will not be further discussed. It is obvious from the academic and political debate that, with these cases, the CJEU opened the door to the neoliberal paradigm. The consequences for workers' and trade unions' rights of such an interpretation of the freedom to provide services and freedom of establishment as has been developed by the CJEU during the last decade are considered to be harmful by many. The case law relating to this matter has been strongly criticized. The pending case of *Sähköalojen ammattiliitto ry*[19] is in line with the abovementioned cases. It deals with the posting of workers and, in particular, the problem of the meaning of minimum rates of pay. It is interesting to note the Advocate General's introductory remark that "the Court has now the opportunity to revisit its extensive body of case-law in this field", i.e. to revisit how to balance the relationship between the freedom of services on the one hand and workers' rights, trade unions' rights, fundamental social rights on the other. The opinion of the Advocate General highlights the critical theoretical analyses of the Court's case law by legal scholars and explicitly says that the existing case law has shifted its focus to the freedom of services.[20] Can we expect a shift in the CJEU's case law towards a more balanced approach?

Another example of the tense relationship between the freedom to provide services and workers' rights and the neoliberal answer to this issue can be seen in the recent CJEU judgment in the case of *Bundesdruckerei GmbH*[21] which addresses the problem of public contracts and special conditions in public tenders. A German company, Bundesdruckerei, applied to the call for tenders for a public contract in the town of Dortmund relating to the digitalization of documents and the conversion of data for the urban planning service of that city. The call contained special conditions demanding that the applicants respect the minimum pay rules; the call for tenders documentation included a standard form to be signed by the contractor, agreeing to pay his employees a minimum hourly wage of €8.62 and to require his subcontractors to comply with that minimum wage as well. Bundesdruckerei argued that this special condition could not be fulfilled by the Polish subcontractor, since minimum wages in Poland are much lower than in Germany. It should be pointed out that the Polish subcontractor was a wholly owned subsidiary of the German company in question.

The Court said, among other things, that "the imposition, under national legislation, of a minimum wage on subcontractors of a tenderer which are established in a Member State other than that to which the contracting authority

16 Case C-341/05 (EU:C:2007:809).

17 Case C-346/06 (EU:C:2008:189).

18 Case C-319/06 (EU:C:2008:350).

19 Case C-396/13; opinion of Advocate General Wahl delivered on 18 September 2014 (EU:C:2014:2236).

20 *Ibid.*, paras. 26, 32.

21 Case 549/13; judgment delivered on 18 September 2014 (EU:C:2014:2235).

belongs and in which minimum rates of pay are lower constitutes an additional economic burden that may prohibit, impede or render less attractive the provision of their services in the host Member State. Consequently, a measure such as that at issue in the main proceedings is capable of constituting a restriction within the meaning of Article 56 TFEU".[22] According to the Court, such a measure cannot be justified and it also appears to be disproportionate. The CJEU's arguments were that such a special condition, which also imposes on the subcontractors from another Member State a fixed minimum wage that bears no relation to the cost of living in the Member State in which the services relating to the public contract are performed "prevents subcontractors established in that Member State from deriving a competitive advantage from the differences between the respective rates of pay" and that "such national legislation goes beyond what is necessary to ensure that the objective of employee protection is attained".[23]

Although a measure which constitutes an additional economic burden and which is therefore capable of constituting a restriction to the freedom of services can be justified according to the CJEU's case law, whereby one of the acceptable justified objectives can be the protection of employees in order to avoid social dumping, the judgment of the Court in the *Bundesdruckerei* case explicitly supported the existence of social dumping. The CJEU's argumentation that it is contrary to the freedom of services to prevent *subcontractors established in another Member State from deriving a competitive advantage from the differences in pay* is in fact a rather good definition of social dumping![24] The competitive advantage is not achieved by better quality or another similar feat, but solely by lower wages paid to the workers of the subcontractor, a wholly owned subsidiary of the applying company, established in another Member State. Such actions directly promote law shopping, social dumping and precarization of work in the entire EU.

Unfortunately, there is no room here to refer to the rest of the recent CJEU case law supporting the same neoliberal trends which result in the increase of precarious work, social dumping and erosion of workers' rights (for example, the *Essent Energie* case[25] and others) or to mention the cases which have the potential to strengthen the protection of vulnerable workers (*Auto-ja Kuljetusalan Työntekijäliitto Akt ry*).[26]

---

22 *Ibid.*, para. 30.

23 *Ibid.*, paras. 32, 33, 34.

24 Especially when one considers the fact that the social dumping is the result of a formal legal manoeuvre of the German company who established a wholly owned subsidiary in Poland.

25 Case C-91/13; judgment delivered on 11 September 2014 (EU:C:2014:2206).

26 Case C-533/13; opinion of Advocate General M. Szpunar delivered on 20 November 2014 (EU:C:2014:2392).

4. FREEDOM OF ESTABLISHMENT AND FREEDOM OF SERVICES VERSUS DIGNITY AT WORK, FUNDAMENTAL SOCIAL RIGHTS AND FREE MOVEMENT OF WORKERS

The posting of workers and, consequently, the problem of social dumping is often addressed as the conflict of interests between the Member States sending out workers (country of origin of the posted worker) and those Member States receiving them (host country, destination country). The benefits of such situations are for the businesses in the countries of origin as well as in the host countries, while the workers of both countries are the losing party. Indeed, it is not merely a conflict between the home and host countries, it is also a conflict of interests between capital and businesses in all countries on the one hand and the workers from the home and host countries on the other hand.

The approach that promotes law shopping and, consequently, the cross-border posting of workers and even the fake posting of workers by setting up letter-box companies, false self-employment and fake cross-border provision of services, results in social dumping. Cremers points out that the "primacy accorded to the freedom of services and the freedom of establishment actually encourages social dumping" and that "posting has become one of the channels for a cross-border recruitment of 'cheap' labour without reference to the rights that can be derived from the EU law pertaining to genuine labour migration".[27]

Such an interpretation of the freedom of services as has been supported by the case law of the CJEU prevents workers from being able to freely move across the EU and find employment in the host Member States. It impedes or renders genuine free movement of workers within the EU, between the Member States less attractive; it impedes the development of a true single European labour market and promotes the segregated national/regional/local labour markets which compete with each other. Companies are not interested in directly employing migrant workers from another Member State who would benefit from the standards related to the free movement of persons within the EU; they prefer to make use of the freedom to establish subsidiaries in another Member State and/or of the institutional framework enabling the posting or hiring of workers from another country at a lower price. This constitutes the downward pressure on the level of workers' rights in all Member States, both home and host countries.

A neoliberal approach supported by the EU policy as well as by the case law of the CJEU results in the (mis)use of the freedom of establishment and

27 J. Cremers, "Letterbox companies and abuse of the posting rules: how the primacy of economic freedoms and weak enforcement give rise to social dumping", ETUI Policy Brief, No 5/2014, ETUI, Brussels 2014, pp. 1, 3.

the freedom of services at the expense of the free movement of workers and the non-discrimination principle, as well as at the expense of workers' rights, fundamental social rights.

There is a tense relationship between the EU economic freedoms on the one side and the fundamental (social) rights and workers' rights on the other side. There is also a tense relationship between the freedom of establishment and the freedom of services on the one hand and the movement of workers on the other. When the economic freedoms prevail both over the fundamental social rights and the right of workers to free movement, which is linked to the prohibition of discrimination, this is the path towards social dumping and gradual erosion of workers' protection. In that case there is no choice for better work, only for cheaper work.

5. HUMAN RIGHTS APPROACH

A different approach, a human rights approach, is possible and necessary. The starting point for this approach is the statement in the ILO Constitution that "labour is not a commodity". Workers are human beings and they have the right to human dignity. It has to be emphasized that such an approach is based on legally binding instruments, i.e. international and European/regional documents on human rights as well as various national constitutions. This means that they are binding and that the Member States as well as the EU have to respect them. The Charter of Fundamental Rights of the European Union,[28] for instance, states the following: "The Union is founded on the indivisible, universal values of human dignity, freedom, equality and solidarity"[29] and "human dignity is inviolable. It must be respected and protected."[30]

The Charter includes numerous fundamental rights, many of which are relevant within the context of work, such as the freedom to choose an occupation and the right to engage in work (Article 15), the right of access to free placement services (Article 29), the right to fair and just working conditions (Article 31) and to protection in the event of unjustified dismissal (Article 30), freedom of association (Article 12), the right of collective bargaining and action (Article 28), workers' right to information and consultation within the undertaking (Article 27) and many other rights, including the fundamental right to liberty and security (Article 6) as well as the right to equality and non-discrimination (Articles 20, 21 and 23).

---

28 OJ C 326, 26.10.2012, pp. 391–407.
29 *Ibid.*, Preamble.
30 Article 1.

However, what should be the EU's response be? Promoting the "free" labour market, or developing labour law in accordance with the standards of human dignity, i.e. in accordance with respect for decent work?

Respect for human rights is one of the EU's main principles, one that has to be abided by in every Member State. If binding legal instruments on human rights are taken seriously, as they should be, the answer is clear.

Labour legislation and labour rights should not be perceived as an obstacle, as a barrier, so that only the minimum, necessary labour regulations are justified. The aim and the potential of labour law is the concretization and realization of human rights in the everyday life of the majority of people who earn a living by working for someone else in a dependent relationship; labour law has the potential to empower people with human dignity.[31] However, this can only be achieved if it guarantees an adequate level of workers' rights and if it applies to all situations in which working people are in need of such protection. Therefore, the goal should be as high a level of workers' protection as possible.

From a human rights perspective, the concept of decent work has to be promoted, instead of "free", "liberalized" and "deregulated" labour market(s). From a human rights perspective, labour law is not rigid if it provides a high level of workers' protection and is well developed. From a human rights perspective, precarious employment conditions are not acceptable.

If a particular (economic) system/regulation is not able to prevent precarization of employment, respect the standards of decent work and guarantee a decent standard of living for everyone, if it does not respect the right to human dignity of working people and fundamental social rights, the system/regulation has to be questioned, not the labour and social rights.

6. CONCLUSION

Fundamental change at the EU level is needed. The neoliberal approach needs to be replaced by a genuine, not just declarative, human rights approach. Is it possible? As yet, this remains to be seen. Nevertheless, the first step towards improvement and change is a clear, critical assessment of the problems. People's awareness that they, as human beings, have the right to decent work, decent lives, decent wages, decent working conditions, etc., and that they can and have to demand these rights is also a necessary (but not sufficient) precondition for a change of the EU policies towards a human rights perspective.

Within the European context (where there is high unemployment, persistent discrimination in (access to) employment and exclusion of particular groups of people and individuals, rising inequalities, in-work poverty, etc.), the most

31 B. Kresal, above n. 6, pp. 150–153.

important issues that should be addressed from a human rights perspective seem to be:

- EU minimum wage regulation;
- reducing working time in full-time employment, limiting overtime work;
- developing decent working conditions in general, within secure employment patterns;[32]
- providing in-work adjustments to change (change as part of progress);[33]
- involvement of workers (reinforcing EU rules on participation in decision-making, participation in profit-sharing);
- promoting transnational/EU collective bargaining;
- effective implementation of workers' rights in practice, with a possibility of seriously considering the establishment of a European labour inspectorate; and
- reinforcing the human rights perspective and the regulation of minimum labour standards at the international level.

Human rights are already established in the binding legal instruments that form the foundations of contemporary societies. They have to be taken seriously and realized in practice in order to bring respect for human dignity into the everyday life of each and every citizen.

32 If there is no adequate and effective protection against dismissal, then all other workers' rights tend to be less efficiently enforced.

33 The focus should be on the internal flexibility instead of on external flexibility. Long-term career development, promoting workers' education, adaptation to changes in people's lives, measures for the reconciliation of work and family responsibilities, etc.

CHAPTER 6

LIMITING THE ROLE OF PUBLIC AUTHORITIES IN THE DEPLOYMENT OF SERVICES

The Tense Relationship between Labour Market Rights and Respect for Dignity at Work, Limiting the Role of Public Authorities in the Deployment of Services*

Gian Guido BALANDI**

1. SOCIAL SERVICES IN GENERAL

Public authorities are in charge of a number of services which influence a large number of aspects of the everyday lives of citizens: from transport to energy, water and gas supply, from childcare to food security control. In this brief report, I will discuss social services, more specifically services provided directly to persons. In the Italian legal system, social services are defined according to a teleological approach: they aim at removing and overcoming needs and difficulties that each person is faced with in the course of life (see Article 128 Act 112/1998 on the transfer of administrative functions and duties from the State to the regions and local authorities).[1]

It is a broad sector, including at least four subsectors. For my reflections here I will take some examples from "services to persons": homecare and residential

* See the ongoing research project *Legal_Frame_Work – Employment and Legality in an Inclusive Society* (a 2010–2011 PRIN research project under Scientific Coordinator Prof. Donata Gottardi), University of Ferrara, Employment and legality in social services unit, coordinator Prof. Gian Guido Balandi.

** Professor of Labour Law, University of Ferrara. The author is particularly grateful to Dr Stefania Buoso for her assistance with this contribution.

1 G. FALCON (ed.), *Lo Stato autonomista: funzioni statali, regionali e locali nel decreto legislativo n. 112 del 1998 di attuazione della legge Bassanini n. 59 del 1997: commento*, Il Mulino, Bologna 1998.

care services.[2] "These services complement and support the role of families in caring for the youngest and oldest members of society in particular", and "persons with long-term health or disability problems".[3]

Note that the research unit I coordinate focuses on the quality of employment of workers in this sector and not the quality of services offered (even if, of course, the quality of the former influences the quality of the latter).

In Italy, the organization of services – in particular social services – can be either public or private.[4]

The competence to regulate social services is divided between the State, the regions and local authorities. After Constitutional Act No 3 of 18 October 2001, the Constitution – see Article 117(m) – declares that "the determination of the basic level of benefits relating to civil and social entitlements has to be guaranteed throughout the national territory". This means that the State has the exclusive competence to guarantee a basic level of benefits in all its territory. The regions have the exclusive competence to organize assistance and social services (ex Article 117.4). At the same time, all public authorities – the State, the regions, metropolitan cities, provinces and municipalities – shall promote the autonomous initiatives of citizens, both as individuals and as members of associations, relating to activities of general interest, based on the principle of subsidiarity (Article 118.4 Const.).

The "legal framework for realizing an integrated system of interventions and social services" is the title of Act No 328/2000.[5] In this Act (Article 1.1), the protection intended for "persons and families" must be achieved in accordance with Articles 2, 3 and 38 of the Constitution: a sort of implicit implementation of solidarity and universal guarantees, deriving from the principle of substantial equality in Article 3.2 Const.[6]

---

2 These are the topics dealt with by the University of Ferrara, more specifically by the research unit working on the project entitled *Legal_Frame_Work – Employment and legality in an inclusive society,* mentioned above. One of the aims of this project is to point out possible regulatory models to promote regular work and fight irregular and informal employment.

3 Commission of the European Communities, *Implementing the Community Lisbon Programme: Social services of general interest in the European Union*, COM (2006) 177 final, p 4.

4 See G.G. Balandi, "'Pubblico', 'privato' e principio di sussidiarietà nel sistema di Welfare State", *RGL*, II, 1998, pp. 213 et seq.

5 Act No 328 of 8 November 2000. See E. Balboni, B. Baroni, A. Mattioni and G. Pastori, *Il sistema integrato dei servizi sociali: commento alla legge n. 328 del 2000 e ai provvedimenti dopo la riforma del titolo V della Costituzione,* Giuffrè, Milan 2007.

6 With a view to foreign readers, it is important to publish the mentioned articles of the Italian Constitution, in the official translation published by Senato della Repubblica: Article 2: "The Republic recognises and guarantees the inviolable rights of the person, both as an individual and in the social groups where human personality is expressed. The Republic expects that the fundamental duties of political, economic and social solidarity be fulfilled". Article 3: "1. All citizens have equal social dignity and are equal before the law, without distinction of sex, race, language, religion, political opinion, personal and social conditions. 2. It is the duty of the Republic to remove those obstacles of an economic or social nature which constrain

The planning and the organization of the "integrated system of actions and social services" falls within the competence of the public authorities (Article 1.3); the role of non-profit organizations of social utility, organizations of cooperation, associations, bodies of social promotion, etc. (Article 1.4) is recognized and facilitated. In Article 5, the Act uses the term "third sector" to include the large and heterogeneous world of non-profit private entities involved in "social affairs".

Therefore, in the sector of social services, public and private organization of the services in question must be integrated in the implementation of the principle of horizontal subsidiarity. According to Article 1.5, public and private entities both ensure the management and provision of social services.

The principle of (horizontal) "social" subsidiarity completes and integrates the institutional subsidiarity: Articles 1.4 and 1.5 explain, complementarily, the respective roles of public and private subjects.

Public subjects in particular must regulate, schedule and organize the management of actions and services in collaboration with private subjects, as they are responsible for the implementation of the right to social assistance (Article 38 Const.).

The social services this research focuses on are childcare and care for the elderly and persons with disabilities.

There is not an EU-wide definition of social services but they are "key instruments for the safeguard of fundamental human rights and human dignity".[7]

The term "personal and household services" covers a broad range of activities that contribute to the well-being of families and individuals at home: childcare and long-term care for the elderly and for persons with disabilities. These types of social services are often provided by social economy actors and play an essential role in maintaining social cohesion. They are generally considered to be in the general interest and are often financed by public budgets; public authorities are involved in the organization and financing of long-term care and childcare as part of their social policies.[8]

---

the freedom and equality of citizens, thereby impeding the full development of the human person and the effective participation of all workers in the political, economic and social organisation of the country". Article 38: "1. Every citizen unable to work and without the necessary means of subsistence is entitled to welfare support. 2. Workers have the right to be assured adequate means for their needs and necessities in the case of accidents, illness, disability, old age and involuntary unemployment. 3. Disabled and handicapped persons are entitled to receive education and vocational training. 4. Responsibilities under this article are entrusted to entities and institutions established by or supported by the State. 5. Private-sector assistance may be freely provided".

7 Commission Communication, *Services of general interest, including social services of general interest: a new European commitment*, COM (2007) 725 final; but also see Article 34 Charter of Fundamental Rights of the EU, "Social Security and Social Assistance".

8 Commission Staff Working Document on exploiting the employment potential of personal and household services, SWD (2012) 95 final.

In 2011, a Eurofound report concluded that informal care providers spend about 80% of their time caring for people with disabilities and this without any impact on public spending whatsoever.

Nevertheless, the number of people employed in the welfare sector has consistently increased, even during the financial crisis: +10.1% in 1995–2011.[9] There is, in particular, a high number of women and immigrants employed in the sector.

2. WHAT IS THE RELATIONSHIP BETWEEN PUBLIC AND PRIVATE SUBJECTS?

Private bodies can become providers of public services through agreements (conventions) or authorizations/accreditations.[10] The first is a contract which is the result of a selection or a discretionary valuation of the administration: see Act 381/1991 on rules about social cooperatives, Article 5 of which regulates the agreements between public authorities and social cooperatives, and Act 266/1991 on a legal framework on the voluntary service, Article 7.

An accreditation is a unilateral act of the administration – usually preceded by an authorization – after it has been confirmed that the private body fulfils the necessary requirements.[11]

Public authorities provide services directly or support provision by private providers (profit or non-profit). However, private providers can also operate on the free market without any connection to the public authorities. Public intervention in the organization and financing of social services is aimed at ensuring the right of all to have access to high-quality services, irrespective of wealth or income, as well as the long-term sustainability of the delivery systems.

While carrying out the abovementioned research, we have found some cases of illegality that have implications both for the public-private management of social services and for the quality of work of employees in both sectors.

---

9 *EU Employment and Social Situation Quarterly Review*, 2014.

10 An authorization aims at realizing structures and exercising the activity of assistance in conformity with regional rules. The entrance of private bodies in the integrated system of actions and social services occurs through accreditation. See S. Frego Luppi, "Il rapporto pubblico – privato e la libertà di scelta dell'utente", in: *Manuale di diritto dei servizi sociali*, Giappichelli, Turin 2011.

11 For a definition of accreditation see Constitutional Court No 416/1995, available at: www.cortecostituzionale.it.

3. THE LIMITATION OF THE ROLE OF PUBLIC AUTHORITIES: EFFECTS AS REGARDS THE CITIZENS

In our experience, but also from a theoretical point of view, the limitation of the role of public authorities in services supply may originate in two different kinds of legislative and/or administrative measures.

Some services are privatized by legislation. Several different instruments may be used to serve this purpose: the abolition or the direct privatization of the public subject that provides the service; the creation of a private subject that provides the same service as the public subject; or the lifting of the ban on private activities in a previously public sector (the abolition of a public monopoly). Below, we shall discuss a number of consequences of these different forms of privatization.

Administrative measures can also remove limitations (seen as "obstacles") to private activities, but the main tool in this field is the so-called "spending review", popularly known as "cuts in public expenditure", which involves the abolishment or outsourcing of some services, entrusting it to private subjects.

Let us consider some consequences of these processes. The first and most important consequence is the transformation of the users from "citizens" to "clients", which means that the relationship between users and suppliers is no longer a political one but a market one. If users, "citizens", are not satisfied with, for instance, the water supply or the organization of nurseries, they can take action using the instruments of democracy. "Clients" can only use market tools, but when the supplier has a monopoly (e.g. water supply) or when the market effect of an increase in demand (a baby boom in a certain area) is an increase in prices, they are simply powerless.

This transformation has a constitutional relevance as well.[12] Every time a constitution determines that the State is responsible for a certain service (which can be expressed as: "the Republic safeguards",[13] "the Republic renders this right effective",[14] or "the State" establishes or supports "entities and institutions"),[15] it is only logical to assume that it is a political and not a market function, and therefore privatizations are presumed to be unconstitutional.

---

12 About the constitutional relevance of the contraposition between Citizen and Consumer, see R. Bin, "Soft Law, No Law", in: A. Somma (ed.), *Soft law e hard law nelle società postmoderne*, Giappichelli, Turin 2009, and R. Bin, "Effettività", in: G. Di Cosimo and L. Lanzalaco (eds.), *Riscoprire la sfera pubblica*, Ati ed., Brescia 2012, p 67.

13 Article 32 deals with "health as a fundamental right of the individual and as a collective interest".

14 Article 34 states that "[c]apable and deserving pupils, including those lacking financial resources, have the right to attain the highest levels of education".

15 To which responsibilities are entrusted regarding the actualization of the rights referred to in Article 38 (social security in every aspect).

If a social service is entrusted to a private undertaking, another important consequence is that the legitimate pursuit of economic profit – which is the normal and lawful function of private enterprises – may create elements of competition as regards the costs of services and not as regards their quality.

Moreover, the reduction of costs may have at least two negative effects. One effect is discrimination against "users". Consider Richard Titmuss' famous phrase, "services for the poor tend to be poor services",[16] which can easily be inverted to say "poor services tend to be services for the poor". This is what can happen when quality is endangered by reducing costs and when there are several undertakings offering the same service; poor and rich – or non-poor – people will receive services of different quality. This can even happen when a public institution and one or several private enterprises are competing against each other.

If the law, or the administrative act that authorizes the private company to supply the public service, corrects this possible discrimination between rich and poor "users" (e.g. universalist service), once again the quality of the services may be at risk. However, if that problem is not remedied, an increase in prices may result in a reduction in the number of users. Only those with an adequate level of income will be able to afford the service in question.

4. EFFECTS OF THE LIMITATION AS REGARDS EMPLOYEES

A second possible effect concerns the workers employed by the "private body" supplying the service. In an effort to reduce costs, the private undertaking may be prompted to apply worse employment terms and conditions: salaries, working hours, etc. This trend is enhanced by the legal provision of the procurement which mentions the principle of "lower costs".[17] This means that if the public administration wants to outsource a service, it could be obliged – under certain circumstances – to contract with the private entity that offers the lowest price or cost. A second negative element is the possibility of (a) sub-procurement chain(s), which typically foster(s) illegality.

In this field, there is a real possibility of social dumping, which can be the result of legal, quasi-legal or even illegal processes. Consider a private undertaking that refers to, and applies, a national collective agreement less

---

16 S.M. Miller, 'The Legacy of Richard Titmuss', in B. Abel-Smith and K. Titmuss (eds.), *The Philosophy of Welfare, Selected Writings of Richard Titmuss*, Allen & Unwin, London 1987, p. 13.

17 See Article 81 entitled "Criteria for the choice of the best offer" of Act No 163/2006 ("Public procurements code"), line 1: the criteria of the "lower price" and of the "most economically advantageous offer". See F. Scarpelli, "Regolarità del lavoro e regole della concorrenza: il caso degli appalti pubblici", *RGL*, IV, 2006, p. 768.

favourable to workers than the one that regulates employment in the public body that outsources the service. Private entities can also conclude local collective agreements that derogate in *peius* from the clauses of the national collective agreements (according to recent legislation, this is now lawful). It is also possible to create *ad hoc* special private entities, such as "social cooperatives" or even "associations of volunteers". These entities – which can be qualified as quasi-legal – can operate with great flexibility as regards employees in every respect: salaries, working time, tasks. In such a scenario, it is not uncommon to come across illegal situations. Undeclared work is widespread in services, particularly when it concerns services to persons.[18] The same goes for so-called "abuse of volunteering", which frequently hides undeclared employment.

All these phenomena are very difficult to keep under control: interventions by labour inspectorates are particularly difficult[19] and sanctions are a highly ineffective deterrence.[20]

Social dumping is also possible in the field of services – liberalized or privatized – as a consequence of the application of the EU principle of freedom of circulation of services. A company that is established in one EU country can offer services to a person in another country under terms and conditions of employment of the home country, a practice that could be tempered by Directive 2014/67, when transposed.[21]

The freedom of circulation of services in the EU opens up an extraordinarily wide field of research.[22] It is well known that services to persons are also included in the freedom of services and that the most recent CJEU case law has favoured the freedom of establishment over labour and social rights. The so-called principle of the "home country", if not tempered by an appreciation of the related risks of "social dumping", may endanger the equilibrium of the labour market in most of the "oldest" members of the Union. This effect, perceived as a sort of "invasion" of alien service providers, has the potential to be politically destructive, as the increase of many anti-European parties has shown. According to Article 3 of the Treaty on European Union, the "internal market" established

---

18 Special Eurobarometer 402, *Undeclared work in the European Union*, 2014; *Documento di programmazione delle attività di vigilanza per l'anno 2013 del Ministero del lavoro – Direzione generale per l'attività ispettiva.*

19 ILO, *Labour Inspection and Undeclared Work in the EU*, Working Document No 29, 2013, p. 14.

20 Eurofound, *Tackling undeclared work in 27 European Union Member States and Norway. Approaches and measures since 2008*, 2013.

21 Directive 2014/67/EU of the European Parliament and of the Council of 15 May 2014 on the enforcement of Directive 96/71/EC concerning the posting of workers in the framework of the provision of services and amending Regulation (EU) 1024/2012 on administrative cooperation through the Internal Market Information System. To be transposed by 18 June 2016.

22 See recent important research in this field in F. Bano, *Diritto del lavoro e libera prestazioni dei servizi nell' Unione Europea*, Il Mulino, Bologna 2008 and G. Orlandini, *Mercato unico dei servizi e tutela del lavoro*, Franco Angeli, Milan 2013.

by the Union "shall work for the sustainable development of Europe based on balanced economic growth [...], a highly competitive social market economy, aiming at full employment and social progress". Is the aggressive circulation of services in line with this programme? There is reason for doubt.

CHAPTER 7

DO WE NEED A NEW CONFLICT-OF-LAWS RULE FOR LABOUR IN THE EUROPEAN ROAD TRANSPORT SECTOR? YES WE DO

Fieke van Overbeeke*

1. INTRODUCTION

In the white book of the Belgian trade unions ABVV and BTB, which came about in collaboration with the University of Antwerp, 25 measures against social dumping in the European road transport sector were presented. One of these measures concerns the adjustment of the current conflict of law rule of Article 8 Rome I Regulation.[1] In this contribution, this measure will be further scrutinized from a labour protection point of view. I will explain why it is necessary to adjust the conflict of law rules to enhance the fight against social dumping in the European road transport sector.

First, a short assessment of the legal framework will be made, which will be followed by an examination of the case law of the Court of Justice of the European Union concerning Article 8 Rome I Regulation. Other mechanisms, such as overriding mandatory rules under Article 9 Rome I Regulation and the Posting of Workers Directive, although relevant for international labour, will not be discussed here as the current focus is on the provision for employment contracts and the specific ABVV-BTB suggestions.[2]

* Teaching and Research Assistant in Private International Law, University of Antwerp.

1 Regulation 593/2008 of the European Parliament and of the Council of 17 June 2008 on the law applicable to contractual obligations (Rome I), *Pb. L* 177/6.

2 Directive 96/71/EC of the European Parliament and of the Council of 16 December 1996 concerning the posting of workers within the framework of the provision of services (Posting of Workers Directive), *Pb. L* 18/1. This directive is directly applicable to cabotage, see Regulation (EC) No 1072/2009 of the European Parliament and of the Council of 21 October 2009 on common rules for access to the international cabotage road haulage market (recast), *Pb.* L 300/72, recital 17. The application of the directive to other forms of international transport (e.g. bilateral transport or cross-trade) depends on whether that specific situation

2. LEGAL FRAMEWORK

2.1. FREEDOM OF SERVICES AND FREEDOM OF ESTABLISHMENT

Key for the realization of the internal market are the fundamental freedoms of circulation. In order to ensure these freedoms in the specific and atypical field of international (road) transport, a common transport policy was created. This policy is defined in Title VI of the Treaty on the Functioning of the European Union (TFEU).[3] Based on this Title, many regulations and directives were enacted, mainly with the aim of increasing the liberalization of the road transport sector.[4] At present, the liberalization is almost complete. Restrictions on the freedom of services ex Article 56 TFEU have been removed, apart from a few restrictions relating to cabotage.[5, 6] The freedom of establishment ex Article 49 TFEU is directly applicable to this sector and is specified in Regulation 1071/2009.[7]

Since labour standards are not harmonized within the Union, it is lucrative for transport companies in low-wage Member States to use the freedom of services to provide cross-border services.[8] Indeed, these low wages and lower labour standards give those companies serious competitive advantages compared to companies located in high-wage Member States.[9] In order to fight this competition, transport companies of high-wage Member States, on the other hand, can use the freedom of establishment (and subsequently the freedom of services) to establish a (letter-box) company in low-wage Member States. These companies are thus able

meets the criteria of the directive. See for this, and more generally for an excellent analysis on the directive and its (poor) interaction with labour in the international (road) transport sector: A. van Hoek and M. Houwerzijl, "'Posting' and 'posted workers' – the need for clear definitions of two key concepts of the Posting of Workers Directive", *Cambridge Yearbook of European Legal Studies* 2014, pp. 435–437.

3 The Treaty of the Functioning of the European Union, *Pb. C* 326/47.

4 See for an overview of the current legislation: Directorate General for Internal Policies – Policy Department B: Structural and Cohesion Policies – Transport and Tourism, "Social and working conditions of road transport hauliers", European Union, 2013.

5 The freedom of services ex Article 56 TFEU is not directly applicable to the (road) transport sector, see Article 58 TFEU. Today, the freedom of services is, in principle, ensured by many regulations.

6 Cabotage is a type of transport which is performed by a vehicle registered in country A, but which only drives in country B. See also Regulation 1072/2009 of the European Parliament and of the Council of 21 October 2009 on common rules for access to the international road haulage market, *Pb. L* 300/72.

7 Regulation 1071/2009 of the European Parliament and of the Council of 21 October 2009 establishing common rules concerning the conditions to be complied with to pursue the occupation of road transport operator and repealing Council Directive 96/26/EC, *Pb. L* 300/51. See Article 5 especially.

8 EU13 Member States are States that entered the Union in 2004, 2007 and 2013.

9 EU15 Member States are the States of the Union before 2004.

to enjoy the low labour costs of the Member State of establishment, even if the lorry drivers are in effect working in EU15 Member States.

Obviously, this legal framework serves as a fertile ground for unfair competition and social dumping. It is, however, questionable whether these (letter-box) constructions truly lead to the avoidance of the higher labour standards of high-wage Member States. Conflict of laws is the field of law that deals with this question.

2.2. CONFLICT OF LAWS – ARTICLE 8 ROME I REGULATION

Conflict of laws is a sub-area of private international law and focuses on the question of which law is applicable in an international legal relationship.[10] The Rome I Regulation harmonizes conflicts of laws relating to contractual obligations within the Union.[11] For international labour relations a specific conflict of law rule was created in Article 8 of the Rome I Regulation. This article has a broad range, as it does not distinguish between different types of labour and thus covers almost every imaginable European labour relation. Hence, labour in European road transport also fits the scope.

Although conflict of laws is traditionally characterized by a neutral and abstract approach, which does not include (social) objectives other than merely appointing the applicable law,[12] the aim of Article 8 is to provide employees with an adequate level of protection.

2.2.1. Article 8(1) Rome I Regulation

Article 8 begins with a choice of law and a subsequent restriction (Article 8(1)). A "choice of law" means that parties can freely choose the law that will govern their contract (the subjectively applicable law). Due to the fact that the employee is the weaker party in the relationship with the employer, this choice is restricted in the sense that the employee cannot be deprived of the protection of provisions laid down in the labour law that is applicable pursuant to Article 8(2), (3) and (4)

---

10 Private international law also focuses on questions relating to international jurisdiction and recognition and enforcement of foreign judgments.

11 The Rome I Regulation replaced the Convention on the law applicable to contractual obligations of 1980 (Rome Convention), *Pb. C* 27/34. The Rome I Regulation applies to contracts concluded after 17 December 2009; see Article 28 Rome I Regulation. With regard to international labour situations both instruments are practically similar.

12 See for example M.-P. Weller, "Anknüpfungsprinzipien im Europäischen Kollisionsrecht: Abschied vond der 'klassischen' IPR-Dogmatik?", *IPRax* 2011, 429–437; Th.M. de Boer, "Prospects for European conflicts law in the twenty-first century", in: P.J. Borchers and J. Zekoll, *International Conflict of Laws for the Third Millennium. Essays in honor of Friedrich. K. Juenger*, N.Y. Transnational Publishers, Ardsley 2001, 193–213.

(the objectively applicable law), i.e. provisions that cannot be derogated from by agreement. Therefore, it remains important to determine the applicable law pursuant to those sections, with or without a choice of law. So in practice, a choice of law in a labour contract does not have much relevance, as the mandatory provisions of the objectively applicable law cannot be avoided.[13]

2.2.2. Article 8(2), (3) and (4) Rome I Regulation

The second layer of protection is provided by the principle of the habitual place of work as the primary connecting factor (Article 8(2)). The law of the country where or from where the employee habitually carries out his or her working activities is applicable, even if the work temporarily takes place in another country.[14] According to the preamble of the Rome I Regulation it is important to take the parties' intention into consideration when interpreting the definition of "temporarily". In practice, however, there are many problems regarding the scope of this definition.[15]

The connecting factor of the engaging place of business only becomes relevant if the habitual place of work cannot be determined (Article 8(3)). The law of the country where the establishment that engaged the employee is located is applicable. In *Voogsgeerd*, the Court made clear that this establishment does not need to have legal personality: the term "place of business" covers every stable structure of an undertaking.[16] This means that not only subsidiaries and branches but also other units, such as the offices of an undertaking, could constitute places of business ex Article 8(3). However, an undertaking has to have a certain degree of permanence, in the exact words of the Court: "the purely transitory presence in a State of an agent of an undertaking from another

---

13 There is discussion about the situation in which a more favourable law is *chosen*. Although this will not occur in practice very often, it is interesting to reflect on this question. In legal literature there is no consensus about this issue. Nevertheless, it can be said that most authors nowadays argue that the chosen (more favourable) law will get priority. See for this latter point of view: Advocate General Trstenjak on 8 September 2011 in the Voogsgeerd Case (C-384/10), No 48. See for an extensive assessment of this discussion: F. van Overbeeke, "Het IPR als instrument ter versterking van de positie van de gedetacheerde werknemer in het web van het vrije verkeer" (PIL as an instrument to reinforce posted workers' position in the web of the fundamental freedoms), *Tijdschrift voor Sociaal Recht* 2013, 699–751.

14 The inclusion of the words "from where" in the Rome I Regulation is new compared to the 1980 Rome Convention. It was, however, already assumed that the Rome Convention should be interpreted in that way, as the Court ruled as such in jurisdiction matters. See CJEU 13 July 1993, C-125/92, *Mulox*, *Jur.*, I, 4075; CJEU 9 January 1997, C-383/95, *Rutten*, *Jur.*, I, 57; CJEU 27 February 2002, C-37/00, *Weber*, *Jur.*, I, 2013.

15 See for an assessment on how to interpret this term: F. van Overbeeke, "Het IPR als instrument ter versterking van de positie van de gedetacheerde werknemer in het web van het vrije verkeer" (PIL as an instrument to reinforce posted workers' position in the web of the fundamental freedoms), *Tijdschrift voor Sociaal Recht* 2013, 699–751.

16 CJEU 15 December 2011, C-384/10, *Jur.* I, 13275, para. 54.

State for the purpose of engaging employees cannot be regarded as constituting a place of business which connects the contract to that state".[17]

Both the habitual workplace principle and the engaging place of business can be deviated from through the so-called "escape clause" (Article 8(4)). This means that if another country is more closely connected to the employment contract, the law of that country is applicable.

2.2.3. A difficult regime applicable to a difficult sector

To recapitulate, Article 8 provides a slightly difficult regime with a restricted choice of law, two connecting factors and a general possibility to deviate from both connecting factors. Besides, the definitions of "provisions that cannot be derogated from by agreement", "habitual workplace", "temporarily", "engaging place of business" and "more closely connected" raise questions about the correct interpretation. Moreover, the exact interrelation between the sections is up for discussion. At the same time, Article 8 has a general regime, applicable to a great variety of international labour situations. Therefore, questions rose about the application of this article to labour in the atypical international road transport sector. In that sector lorry drivers are very mobile, working in and across many countries. How then to determine the applicable labour law to these drivers? Fortunately, the Court answered, or at least tried to answer, this question in the famous *Koelzsch* case of 2011.[18]

3. CASE LAW OF ARTICLE 8 ROME I REGULATION

First, I will discuss the *Koelzsch* case; subsequently, the *Voogsgeerd* case will be dealt with. As will become clear, the latter case confirms the *Koelzsch* case, although the Court's explanation of how to interpret the "engaging place of business" in Article 8(3) is also interesting. I will conclude the assessment of both cases with a provisional review. This will be followed by an examination of the *Schlecker* case.[19] After the discussion of this "trio" of cases, the effect of Article 8 on the European transport sector can be measured. It will become clear that Article 8 and the subsequent case law are insufficient to deal with social dumping problems in that sector.

---

17 *Ibid.*, para. 55.

18 CJEU 15 March 2011, C-29/10, *Jur.* I, 1595. Strictly, the *Koelzsch* case (and the other two cases of *Voogsgeerd* and *Schlecker* that will be discussed in this contribution) still concerned the 1980 Rome Convention that was replaced by the Rome I Regulation. As mentioned before, the regimes relating to labour are practically similar. Therefore, and for reasons of readability, I will only refer to Article 8 when assessing these cases.

19 CJEU 12 September 2013, C-64/12, *Schlecker* (not yet published in *Jur.*).

3.1. *KOELZSCH* CASE – BROAD HABITUAL WORKPLACE PRINCIPLE

The *Koelzsch* case, which was handled by the Grand Chamber of the Court, is a key case for the interpretation of Article 8. It concerned a German lorry driver, Mr Koelzsch, who drove flowers from Germany to Denmark. Koelzsch lived in Germany, the lorries were located there and he also received his assignments there. However, he signed the employment contract at a subsidiary of his employer in Luxembourg, a choice of law was made for Luxembourg law and the social security was regulated by Luxembourg law as well.

After a dispute between Koelzsch and his employer, the question arose as to which labour law was applicable to the employment contract.[20] Some scholars assumed that the "engaging place of business" of Article 8(3) was *par excellence* written for lorry drivers, as these drivers work in and across many different countries.[21] It was argued that one needed imagination to determine a habitual place of work for these highly mobile lorry drivers. The Court, however, disagreed and ruled that even when an employee carries out his activities in more than one State, the habitual workplace principle applies as far as possible to determine the applicable labour law. The Court explicitly highlighted the need for a "broad interpretation" of the habitual workplace principle and mainly underpinned this by the fact that the objective of Article 8 is to guarantee an adequate protection for the employee. Therefore, this provision must be understood, in the words of the Court, "as guaranteeing the applicability of the law of the State in which he carries out his working activities, rather than that of the State in which the employer is established".[22]

As far as road transport is concerned, the Court also provided some linking factors specifically relevant to that sector, namely: the place from which the employee carries out his transport tasks, receives instructions concerning his tasks and organizes his work; the place where his work tools are situated, where the transport is principally carried out, where the goods are unloaded and where the employee returns to after completion of his tasks.[23] Hereafter, I will refer to these elements as the "*Koelzsch* elements".

---

20 As stated above, this question remains relevant, notwithstanding the choice of law for Luxembourg law.

21 See for example: A.T.J.M. Jacobs and E.J.M. van Herk, "Sociale aspecten van Europese liberalisering van het beroepsgoederenvervoer over de weg", *Sociaal Economisch Weekblad* 1995, 155–170.

22 CJEU 12 September 2013, C-64/12, *Schlecker*, paras. 40–44.

23 *Ibid.*, para. 49.

3.2. *VOOGSGEERD* CASE – CONFIRMATION

A few months later, the Court unambiguously confirmed this broad interpretation of the habitual workplace principle in the *Voogsgeerd* case, but then in relation to transport by sea. The dispute was centred on the port of Antwerp. Mr Voogsgeerd worked as a chief engineer on a ship that boarded at Antwerp and whose navigation area extended across the North Sea. The owner of the ship and the formal employer (i.e. the employer according to the employment contract) of Voogsgeerd was Navimer, established in Luxembourg. However, the employment contract was signed at the headquarters of Naviglobe NV in Antwerp, of which Navimer was a subsidiary. It was also at Naviglobe that Voogsgeerd in effect performed most of his working activities, e.g. he received instructions from Naviglobe and returned to Naviglobe after each voyage. Similar to the *Koelzsch* case, a choice of law was made for the law of Luxembourg.

With regard to Naviglobe, Voogsgeerd argued that Belgian labour law was applicable ex Article 8(3), as the engaging place of business should be interpreted as the business to which the employee is connected for his *actual employment*. The Court rightly pointed out the fact that Article 8(3) is, at first glance, not relevant in this situation, as the workplace principle in Article 8(2) should be examined first. In that context, the Court repeated and confirmed the ruling of the *Koelzsch* case, as it stated that the workplace principle must be interpreted broadly.[24]

Subsequently, the Court made it clear that elements pertinent to the "actual employment" are not relevant when determining the applicable labour law pursuant to Article 8(3), as those elements already play a role in the workplace principle in Article 8(2). According to the Court, only matters purely relating to "the conclusion of the contract" should be taken into account, such as "the place of business which published the recruitment notice and that which carried out the recruitment interview".[25] The Court thus opts for a narrow interpretation of the "engaging place of business", in which the term exclusively refers to the place of business which engaged the employee and not to the place to which the employee is connected through his actual employment.

3.3. PROVISIONAL REVIEW

3.3.1. *Broad interpretation desirable to mitigate bold flag out operations*

The *Koelzsch* and *Voogsgeerd* cases are to be welcomed in terms of the broad interpretation of the workplace principle, especially regarding the current social

24 *Ibid.*, paras. 32–36.
25 *Ibid.*, paras. 46–50.

dumping situation in the European road transport sector. It has been made clear once and for all that in the cases of lorry drivers, the habitual workplace principle is the main criterion too when the applicable labour law has to be determined. This means that the sole relocation of a (transport) company does not automatically mean that the labour law of the new place of establishment applies. Since cheap labour costs are one of the most important incentives for relocating companies to low-wage countries, the judgments in these cases certainly make these operations less attractive.[26] More specifically, if a Belgian transport company establishes a letter-box company in Hungary and hires Hungarian employees who will subsequently be sent to Belgium to work, in principle Belgian labour law applies pursuant to Article 8(2).

3.3.2. Still, not a solution

However, most transport cases are not that easy. The *Koelzsch* case was very particular and many factors could easily be linked to Germany: Mr Koelzsch was German, he lived there, he received his instructions there, the working tools (lorries) were there, he departed from and returned to Germany, etc. In that light, Mr Koelzsch can in fact be seen as a kind of bus driver, but for flowers.[27]

In practice, however, many constructions that are set up in the transport sector to avoid the applicable labour law are different and more sophisticated than the law-avoiding factual situation in *Koelzsch*. Think for example of a situation in which company X, established in a low-wage Member State, is taken over by company Y, established in a high-wage Member State, with the sole purpose of performing transport tasks for company Y. The lorry drivers of company X are transported to company Y with minivans for the duration of six to eight weeks. During that period, they drive across Europe, without returning to company Y. They live, sleep and work in their lorries, while driving to and from different establishments (or customers) of company Y in Europe, where they also receive new instructions. After final completion of the tasks, they are picked up by a minivan (whether or not in another Member State than the one

---

26 See for the possible interrelation between the freedom of services and establishment: V. Van Den Eeckhout, "Internationaal arbeidsrecht gemangeld tussen Europese fundamentele vrijheden", *Tijdschrift Recht en Arbeid* 2009, 32; V. Van Den Eeckhout, "Enkele beschouwingen naar aanleiding van diverse recente Europese en Nederlandse uitspraken in het internationaal arbeidsrecht (Koelzsch, Voogsgeerd, Vicoplus, Nuon-rechtspraak en zaak FNV/De Mooij). Welke (nieuwe) argumentatiemogelijkheden voor werknemers tot opeisen van (meer) arbeidsrechtelijke bescherming in internationale situaties?", *ARBAC* 2012, 19; F. van Overbeeke, "The habitual workplace and the freedom of establishment in international transport", in the upcoming Jean Monnet Lifelong Learning series 2015. See for the interrelation between labour migration in a broad sense, the contribution of H. Verschueren in this book.

27 As Professor B. Barentsen (University of Leiden, the Netherlands) entertainingly puts it in his colleges.

where company Y is established) and brought back to their home States. After two weeks they are, once again, transported from company X to company Y and the cycle restarts. It needs to be stressed that this example is not a theoretical one, as inspection reports and court cases in the Member States show that this is common practice in the transport sector.[28]

Obviously, the determination of a "habitual workplace" is much more difficult in this situation than it was in the *Koelzsch* case. In practice, this question is therefore often the most debated one, even in cases where the elements can be linked more easily to a certain country.

The consequences of failing to determine a habitual place of work can be unfavourable to lorry drivers. As stated above, in those cases the regime of Article 8 induces a reversion to the engaging place of business in Article 8(3). As a result of the Court's narrow approach of this definition in *Voogsgeerd*, the place of business where (most of) the elements relating to the conclusion of the contract can be found will be considered the main place of establishment: in practice this could easily lead to the establishment in a low-wage Member State.[29] So it could have been more favourable for employees if the Court had followed Mr Voogsgeerd (and the intervening Belgian government) in his reasoning that elements regarding the "actual employment" are relevant in the application of Article 8(3). Obviously, the same elements should not have a double function in Article 8(2) and (3), but are these elements genuinely the same? The element of the *de facto* place of business of the employer (where the actual employment takes place) is not included in the interpretation of the habitual place of work, although it would have affected the "engaging place of business" in the interpretation of Voogsgeerd. I agree that certain *Koelzsch* elements, such as the place from which the employee carries out his transport tasks, the place where his work tools are and the place to which the employee returns after completion of his tasks, could be the same as the *de facto* place of business. However, as was mentioned above, in practice there could be fierce discussion on the application of the (broad) workplace principle and the *Koelzsch* elements. Would it not be better, from a labour protection perspective, if the Court had agreed with Mr Voogsgeerd and a "second chance" could be given to the interpretation of the "engaging place of business"; and this, by taking into account the element of the *de facto* place of business where the actual employment takes place (in such a way that this element could play a decisive role when it is impossible to locate a habitual place of work)? In my opinion it would.

---

28 See for example the Dutch documentary made by the Dutch trade union FNV in Zembla of 12 December 2012 (YouTube).

29 Indeed, it is often at that place that lorry drivers are recruited, the recruitment notice is published and the recruitment interview is carried out.

3.3.3. *Risk of an incorrect interpretation of the Koelzsch elements – Ryanair case*

This is all the more relevant given the risk of an incorrect application of the *Koelzsch* elements by the national courts. This can be seen, for example, in the *Ryanair* case, which is notorious in Belgium, where a Belgian labour court made extraordinarily poor use of the *Koelzsch* elements.[30] In brief, the case concerned the airline company Ryanair, which has its headquarters in Ireland and a subsidiary in Belgium. Ryanair flew its personnel, who were recruited in Belgium, to Ireland to officially have the recruitment interview there and to subsequently conclude the employment contract there (with a choice of law for Irish law). In reality, the employees were only working in and from Belgium. According to the *Koelzsch* elements, Belgium was the place from which the employees carried out their transport tasks, received instructions concerning the tasks, organized their work, where the work tools were and to which the employees returned after completion of their tasks. The Belgian labour court explicitly agreed with this by summing up and linking all these elements to Belgium, except for the place where the work was organized. According to the labour court the headquarters are located in Ireland since all flights, departures, etc. are organized from that place. Therefore, and this was the final ruling of the labour court, the habitual place of work cannot be Belgium, as Belgium was not "*prépondérante*" (preponderant) here in the way Germany was in the *Koelzsch* case.[31]

In my view, there are three essential flaws in this reasoning. Firstly, the linking factor of the place where the work is organized does not refer to the place where the *employer* organizes the work, but where the *employee* organizes his work. Secondly, not all the linking factors have to point to one singular State to constitute a habitual place of work: these factors are not cumulative but indicative. Thirdly, it is not necessary for one country to be preponderant as the habitual place of work. The Court of Justice does not even use the word preponderant: instead, the Court states that the work should have a "*rattachement significatif*" (a significant connection) with a State, which in my view is a less stringent criterion than preponderant.

This lower court case thus perfectly illustrates the variety of mistakes that can occur by applying the *Koelzsch* elements. In that light, the rejection of the Court in *Voogsgeerd* of the possible "second chance" at establishing the engaging place of business is all the more inconvenient. In fact, if this second chance had

---

30 Judgment of 2 September 2013, Tribunal du Travail de Charleroi – *X v. Ryanair*, see www.eurprocedure.be. Strictly, the dispute first concerned the question whether the Belgian court was internationally competent to deal with the case. However, the labour tribunal explicitly used the *Koelzsch* elements here. See also: G. Van Calster, "Ceci n'est pas une base Ryanair?", *De Juristenkrant* 2013, 4; F. Hendrickx, "Actualiteit. Vliegende arbeidsvoorwaarden", *RW* 2013–14, 1242.

31 In the exact words of the labour tribunal: "*Alors que dans l'arrêt Koelzsch, l'Allemagne était prépondérante, ici n'est pas possible de considérer que la Belgique est prépondérante.*"

been accepted, I believe that in the *Ryanair* case Belgian law would have been considered to be the applicable labour law, Belgium being the country where the actual employment took place, which could have been decisive in this matter. The Court's current narrow interpretation in *Voogsgeerd* now has the opposite effect, namely the applicability of Irish labour law (which is exactly what *Ryanair* wanted).

3.3.4. Possibilities through the escape clause?

However, it should be mentioned that in *Voogsgeerd* the Court also pointed out the escape clause of Article 8(4), which enables a deviation from the, possibly rigid, result of the narrow approach. In that way, perhaps the applicability of Irish law pursuant Article 8(3) in the abovementioned hypothesis concerning the *Ryanair* case could have been deviated from on the basis that Belgium would be the more closely connected country. This openly and vaguely formulated "connecting factor", however, causes legal uncertainty for both the employer and the employee. Moreover, the recent *Schlecker* case shows us that this escape clause is purely based on the *nearest connection principle*, which is not to be interpreted through elements of labour protection but merely through neutral elements. As will become clear from the assessment of this case in section 3.4, this could turn out to be unfavourable in terms of the protection of lorry drivers and constitutes an important argument to adjust the current conflict of laws rule of Article 8.

3.3.5. Summary

So, on the one hand, the broad interpretation of the habitual workplace principle in *Koelzsch* and *Voogsgeerd* is favourable when it comes to labour protection in lorry driver cases. At least, the Court did not pick the engaging place of business as the primary connecting factor when it comes to determining the applicable labour law in the cases of lorry drivers. On the other hand, this broad interpretation only affects manifest law-avoiding constructions (such as the establishment of a letter-box company), or rather simple cases such as the *Koelzsch* case. As for other, more sophisticated constructions, it remains hard to determine the applicable law pursuant to the habitual workplace principle. In those situations, the danger of a reversion to the engaging place of business occurs. On the basis of the Court's narrow interpretation of the "engaging place of business" in *Voogsgeerd*, this could easily lead to the applicability of the law of a low-wage Member State. From a labour protection perspective, the Court should have accepted the "actual employment" interpretation of *Voogsgeerd*. This connecting factor could then have served as a "second chance", which is not a bad idea considering the difficulties that arise from determining a habitual place of work for lorry drivers and the risk of an incorrect interpretation. The

Belgian *Ryanair* case illustrates this perfectly. However, due to the escape clause of Article 8(4), it is still possible to deviate from a possibly rigid result that was achieved by applying Article 8(3). Unfortunately, the Court interpreted this escape clause in a formalistic and not particularly labour-friendly way.

3.4. *SCHLECKER* CASE – QUALIFICATION OF THE REASONING OF THE COURT IN *KOELZSCH*

Given the broad interpretation of the workplace principle in *Koelzsch* and *Voogsgeerd*, with the main argument that this broad interpretation complies with the objective of Article 8 (which is to provide adequate protection for the employee), the question arose whether and to what extent a deviation was still possible when the applicable labour law could be determined on the basis of the habitual workplace principle. Indeed, if the labour law of the country in which the habitual place of work is located guarantees an adequate level of protection, the requirements of the objective of Article 8 are met, whether or not this is the most favourable outcome in the case in question. Therefore, a deviation via Article 8(4) could be in conflict with this objective. The Court, however, disagreed and ruled that such a deviation is still possible, even when an employee carries out the work for a long period and without interruption in the same country. This is mainly underpinned by the reasoning that the guarantee of adequate protection for the employee is reflected in the idea that the law of the country that is *most closely connected* to the case should apply.[32]

The Court also provides some "significant factors suggestive of a connection with a particular country" that should be taken into account: "the country in which the employee pays taxes on the income from his activity and the country in which he is covered by a social security scheme and pension, sickness insurance and invalidity schemes [...] the parameters relating to salary determination and other working conditions".[33]

Confusingly, the Court adds a nuance to this, as it ruled that a deviation from Article 8(2) cannot automatically occur solely because the other relevant circumstances *by dint of their number* would result in the selection of another country. So, on the one hand, it is not the habitual workplace principle that offers the best guarantee of adequate protection, but the closest connection principle, in which the habitual place of work apparently is "just" a presumption. On the other hand, however, one still cannot deviate from the habitual workplace principle on the basis of the number of circumstances. In my view, it is precisely the number of circumstances that would lead to another more closely connected country, which, according to the Court, in the end guarantees adequate

32 Judgment of 2 September 2013, Tribunal du Travail de Charleroi – *X v. Ryanair*, para. 34.

33 *Ibid.*, para. 41.

protection. The Court thus seems to contradict itself, as the added nuance still renders a certain pertinence to the workplace principle.

However, if the Court's ruling were to be applied to the specific circumstances of the *Schlecker* case, it would presumably lead to a deviation from the easily located habitual place of work, where the employee worked for over eleven years. The case concerned a German frontier worker, Ms Boedeker, who was employed by the German company Schlecker. The company had branches in several Member States. After working in a branch in Germany for almost fifteen years, Boedeker was sent to a branch in the Netherlands. She continued living in Germany and remained on the German social security scheme as well. She had been working in the Netherlands for approximately eleven years when she received a notification of the abolishment of her function in the Netherlands and was sent to a branch in Germany. After a dispute, the employer argued that German law was applicable ex Article 8(4), as that law was more closely connected to the case. Obviously, the habitual place of work can be located in the Netherlands, as that was the only place where the employee had been working. Nevertheless, all the other elements pointed to Germany, and given the judgment of the Court (notwithstanding the added nuance), it seems that in that situation a deviation was justified, favouring the (less protective) German law.

3.4.1. Evaluation – effect on road transport situations?

A lot can be said about this case. Without reverting to highly technical conflict of laws discussions on principles of conflict of laws and how to interpret Article 8 in that light,[34] I will attempt to assess the effect of this judgment on European road transport cases.

Apparently, the overarching principle of Article 8 is to link the employment contract to the country that constitutes the closest connection. Neutral elements are taken into consideration when interpreting this closest connection. However, this does not necessarily include labour-friendly elements. Pursuant to that view, the habitual workplace principle is "just" a presumption of the closest connected country and can therefore be deviated from if this presumption does not lead to this closest connected country. Although it is uncertain whether this is actually the correct interpretation, particularly given the fact that the Court was seated in the Grand Chamber in the *Koelzsch* case and in the Third Chamber in the *Schlecker* case, I will henceforth assume that this interpretation is the proper one.

From a labour protection perspective this case could have highly undesirable effects on the international road transport situation. As mentioned earlier, there are already many difficulties when it comes to locating a habitual place of work

---

34 This will be discussed in my PhD thesis on labour protection and constructions to avoid the applicable labour law in the road transport sector (still in progress).

in transport cases. These difficulties are inherent to the job of an international lorry driver, who is driving in, from and across many countries in often short periods of time. Even *if* the habitual place of work *can* in fact be located in those circumstances, the employer is *still* able to deviate from it through the escape clause. Firstly, the employer could, for instance, strongly contest the habitual place of work. Secondly, it could be argued that if a habitual place of work can be determined, it is still possible to deviate from this. Thus, especially in the cases of lorry drivers, where it is already difficult to determine the habitual place of work as elements are scattered everywhere, these possible arguments are strong and particularly inconvenient when it comes to the rights of lorry drivers. I call this the "*Schlecker* effect".

However, the question whether the *Schlecker* case directly affects lorry drivers still remains, as the case concerned a particular frontier worker situation, *not* a transport situation.[35] On the other hand, I do not see why this case could not apply to transport situations too since the Court provided some general remarks concerning Article 8(4). Anyway, in practice this case provides powerful armour to employers in their argumentation to apply the law of low-wage countries. In fact, the Schlecker case has already been used to try to seduce national courts to deviate from a habitual place of work.[36]

4. FINAL REMARKS

In this contribution the effect of the conflict of laws rule of Article 8 Rome I Regulation on the European road transport sector is assessed. This is done purely from a labour protection perspective. In that context, the *Koelzsch* and *Voogsgeerd* cases are to be welcomed in the sense that the Court prescribed a broad interpretation of the habitual workplace principle and explicitly applied it to transport situations. The *Koelzsch* elements are also useful in the attempt to locate a habitual place of work for highly mobile lorry drivers. The *Koelzsch* case in particular seems to be one of the first clear signs that the Court is concerned about the current social problems in that sector. However, the localization of a habitual place of work for lorry drivers is still problematic in more sophisticated law-avoiding constructions. In that situation the failure to determine a habitual place of work is "sanctioned" by a reversion to the connecting factor of the engaging place of business. Although the Court cannot be held accountable for

---

35 See also for the particularities of the case: V. Van Den Eeckhout, "De ontsnappingsclausule van artikel 6 lid 2 slot EVO Verdrag (artikel 8 lid 4 Rome I Verordening): Hoe bijzonder is de zaak Schlecker? 12 September 2013, C-64/12, Schlecker/Boedeker (The Escape-Clause of Article 6 Rome Convention (Article 8 Rome I Regulation): How Special Is the Case Schlecker?)", *Tijdschrift Recht en Arbeid* 2014.

36 This can be seen in the pending Dutch case: *FNV v. Van Den Bosch Transporten* (will be made public on www.rechtspraak.nl if the case is closed).

this consequence, as it is the legislator that creates the rules and thus created the secondary connecting factor in the first place, the Court could at least have mitigated this consequence in the *Voogsgeerd* case where it had to answer the question on how to interpret this connecting factor. The Court explicitly rejected the "second chance" after a failure to determine the habitual place of work, with a possible decisive role for the *de facto* place of business where the actual employment takes place. This could easily result in the applicable labour law being the law of a low-wage country. Although I agree that the interpretation of the Court ensures some legal certainty, the Court does not seem to care too much about that in the *Schlecker* case: legal uncertainty is inherent to the fact that there are still possibilities to deviate from an already located habitual place of work.

Besides, the *Schlecker* case seems to contain a nuance missing in the *Koelzsch* case. Apparently, the Court is of the opinion that the thesis that labour protection is best guaranteed by a broad workplace principle needs to be altered to the idea that it is primarily the closest connection principle that ensures this main objective of Article 8. The habitual place of work is then just an assumption. Moreover, it seems that merely neutral elements affect the closest connection principle. Especially in the road transport sector, where linking factors are scattered, this could turn out to be highly unfavourable in terms of the labour protection of lorry drivers, referred to in this contribution as the "*Schlecker* effect".

Consequently, the creation of a new conflict of laws rule that is applicable to the special and atypical field of labour in the European road transport sector is recommended. This could be done in different ways. For example, the *Koelzsch* elements could be explicitly included in the workplace principle, as the ABVV-BTB white book suggests. Another option would be to adopt a separate regulation or directive, specifically tailored to the road transport sector. It could adopt special connecting factors, without maybe even using the workplace principle. At the very least, the engaging place of business as interpreted by the Court should be abolished.[37] In that way the risk of reverting to the engaging place of business is eliminated. Besides the adoption of new, or the abolishment of old, conflict of law rules, there should be a simultaneous reflection on whether some predetermined overriding mandatory rules should be added. These rules could then be applicable, regardless of the objectively or subjectively applicable labour law. Inspiration could be taken from the Posting of Workers Directive, which already contains such mandatory rules for posted workers.[38]

---

37 See also U. Grusic, "Should the connecting factor of the 'engaging place of business' be abolished in European Private International Law?", *International and Comparative Law Quarterly* 2013, pp. 173–192, but especially in the context of international jurisdiction.

38 The Posting of Workers Directive leads to many difficulties in practice. However, the system itself – which provides predetermined overriding mandatory rules – could also be suitable for

The social problems in the European road transport sector are too diverse for cut-and-dried answers. However, that does not mean that the current situation cannot be improved. An amendment of the rules of the sometimes forgotten field of conflict of laws could contribute to the fight against social dumping. If we take the various fields of law together and explore the possibilities to adjust them in such a way that social rights are taken more seriously, a slightly more social Europe might not be as infeasible as it currently seems.

---

the road transport sector. It can offer certainty concerning the application of a certain level of minimum social protection.

CHAPTER 8
THE RIGHT TO HUMAN DIGNITY: ULTIMATE LIMIT TO SOCIAL COMPETITION AND MARKET FREEDOMS

Ferran Camas Roda*

1. INTRODUCTION

In the light of the labour market reforms currently being carried out in Europe, the symposium "From social competition to social dumping. The workers' right to human dignity at stake", organized by Prof. Dr Marc Rigaux of the University of Antwerp on 20–21 November 2014, could not have come at a better time.

The changes in labour law and labour law policy at the European level may be affecting the workers' right to dignity in employment relations, whose origins, in terms of law, date back to the nineteenth century. It is my belief that respect for the principle of human dignity is of the utmost importance if we want to avoid the negative effects of these labour law reforms on workers' standard of living.

In this contribution, I will focus on the principle of human dignity as laid down in the Charter of Fundamental Rights and in the Treaties of the European Union. I will also refer to declarations or background documents of related legislation in the Union.

I will end this contribution by emphasizing the need to incorporate human dignity as a transversal principle of labour law and the exercise of fundamental rights and the Community freedoms derived from it. To this end, I will argue that the dignity of workers must be a dogmatic concept to be used against the economy-oriented theories that are reshaping the workers' rights, and also that the value of human dignity is intrinsic to the economic liberties presented in the constitutional treaties of the European Union.

* Full Professor of Labour and Social Security Law and Director of the Chair of Immigrations, Rights and Citizenship, University of Girona.

2. HUMAN DIGNITY IN THE CHARTER OF FUNDAMENTAL RIGHTS OF THE EUROPEAN UNION

In the preamble to the Charter, human dignity is referred to as one of the indivisible, universal values upon which the Union is founded. By establishing the citizenship of the Union and by creating an area of freedom, security and justice, it (and I quote) "places the individual at the heart of its activities".

Not only do these foundations possess supporting or legitimizing characteristics, they also govern the actions of the Union. In other words, they constitute the criteria and guidelines for the actions of the EU institutions. Moreover, this also explains why in Article 21 of the Consolidated Version of the Treaty of the European Union, respect for human dignity is specified as a requirement for EU action in the international arena. In other words, the Treaty directly links the European Union's foreign policy actions to respect for human dignity.[1]

The preamble also states that the Charter reaffirms, with due regard for the powers and tasks of the Union and for the principle of subsidiarity, the rights resulting from the constitutional traditions and international obligations common to the Member States, the European Convention for the Protection of Human Rights and Fundamental Freedoms, the Social Charters adopted by the Union and by the case law of the Court of Justice of the European Union and of the European Court of Human Rights.

Regarding the European Convention for the Protection of Human Rights and Fundamental Freedoms, the generic rights contained therein can be applied to the work environment in general, although as far as rights specifically related to work are concerned, it regulates the prohibition of slavery, servitude, forced labour and discrimination. It also regulates trade union rights within the framework of the freedom of association, which specifically mentions the right to form and join trade unions. As the European Court of Human Rights stated on 29 April 2002 (in *Pretty v. the UK*), the right to human dignity is a founding principle which underlies and guides the entire Convention, pointing out that "the very essence of the Convention is respect for human dignity and human freedom".

In 1961, with a view to addressing the previous Convention's shortcomings in social matters, the European Council adopted the European Social Charter, which includes a comprehensive list of social rights, many of which may be directly and fully implemented in the workplace.[2] However, in the revised

1 P. Serna, "Dignidad humana", in: E. Álvarez Conde and V. Garrido Mayol, *Comentarios a la Constitución Europea*, Libro II, Tirant lo Blanch, 2004, pp. 191–240.

2 C. Alfonso Mellado, "El Derecho del Trabajo. Referentes constitucionales e internacionales", *Fundación 1 de Mayo: Colección Estudios*, No 75, October 2013.

version of the Charter, formulated in 1996, express mention of human dignity in the workplace is made, establishing in Article 26 the right of all workers "to dignity at work". This means that the signing parties undertake to promote certain actions to prevent sexual harassment in the workplace as well as recurrent reprehensible or distinctly offensive actions directed against individual workers in the workplace or in relation to work.

Finally, the preamble of the Charter expresses that the Union recognizes the rights, freedoms and principles set out thereafter and proceeds with the list of articles, the first title being dedicated to dignity. Article 1 states that: "[h]uman dignity is inviolable. It must be respected and protected."

Subsequently, also under Title 1, it is recognized that "[n]o one shall be required to perform forced or compulsory labour" (Article 5).

As an initial conclusion, we can assert that by naming the first title "Dignity" and by referring to human dignity in its first section, it was the intention of the Convention that drafted the Charter to establish a special link between human dignity and the rights included under this title (the right to life, to the integrity of the person), and, directly related to work, the prohibition of forced labour.

As to whether it is a value, a principle or a right, it must be said that the Charter has not only positioned human dignity as an indivisible, universal right on which the Union has been founded, but by including it in the regulatory section of articles, has also framed it as a fundamental right of the Union.[3]

Later on, Title IV of the Charter regulates the workers' right to information and consultation within the undertaking, the right of collective bargaining and action, protection in the event of unjustified dismissal, the right of all workers to fair and just working conditions, the prohibition of child labour and protection of young people at work, the protection of family and professional life, social security and social assistance, access to health care, environmental protection, consumer protection and access to services of general economic interest.

It should be emphasized that all these rights in the Charter come under the heading of "Solidarity". Firstly, giving this name to Title IV has raised it to the status of a legal principle which, like human dignity, has resulted in rights and responsibilities, especially the ones that are covered by this title.

Secondly, it is necessary to mention Supiot, who, referring to the general notion of solidarity within the framework of social rights, said that its main goal is to establish a container in the heart of the community in which everyone should place what they can and take out what they need, adding that the obligation assumed by every individual to contribute to the protection of all persons has its origins in the Duties of Man, implicitly or explicitly recognized by declarations on fundamental rights.[4]

---

3 P. Serna, "Dignidad humana", in: E. Álvarez Conde and V. Garrido Mayol, *Comentarios a la Constitución Europea*, Libro II, Tirant lo Blanch, 2004, pp. 191–240.

4 A. Supiot, *L'esprit de Philadelphie. La justice sociale face au marché total.* Paris, Seuil, 2010.

The naming of the principle of solidarity in Title IV implies a social nature is assigned to the rights it contains. Arising from these, and for each of the subsections, are the rights and duties towards one's fellows and the group to which one belongs. The recognition and effectiveness of these social rights cannot be defined on an individual level, that is based exclusively on the authority of the undertaking to regulate working conditions or on the agreements stemming from the freedom of action of both parties to implement the rights laid down in Title IV of the Charter, but must be based on the principle of solidarity that protects them. These laws should be interpreted in collective and social terms so that, in their implementation, the protection of the weaker party comes first.

These criteria should underlie the implementation of the rights laid down in Title IV of the Charter and, in particular, in Article 31, which makes the only reference under this title to dignity in the workplace. The first part of this rule, aimed specifically at regulating "fair and just working conditions", establishes that "every worker has the right to working conditions which respect his or her health, safety and dignity".

According to Title VII, regarding general provisions governing the interpretation and application of the Charter, in particular in Article 51, which is aimed at regulating its scope of implementation, "the provisions of this Charter are addressed to the institutions, bodies, offices and agencies of the Union, with due regard for the principle of subsidiarity and to the Member States only when they are implementing Union law. They shall therefore respect the rights, observe the principles and promote the application thereof in accordance with their respective powers and respecting the limits of the powers of the Union as conferred on it in the Treaties".

To sum up, the provisions of the Charter are addressed to the institutions and bodies of the EU, with due regard for the principle of subsidiarity and to the Member States only when they are implementing Union law. This means that the Charter is not made up of a set of fundamental rights enforceable against the internal regulations of each State, but rather of a set of rights limited to the area of the European Union.[5]

Respect and protection of human dignity is addressed to the entities laid down in Article 51, in other words, to the institutions, bodies and offices of the Union and to the Member States only when they are implementing Union law. Mention must also be made of the Constitution of the Republic of Poland, in relation to the Charter of Fundamental Rights of the European Union valid in the Consolidated Version of the Treaty on European Union 2012, which says that "the Charter does not affect in any way the right of Member States to legislate in the sphere of public morality, family law, as well as the protection of human dignity and respect for human physical and moral integrity".

---

[5] C. Alfonso Mellado, "El Derecho del Trabajo. Referentes constitucionales e internacionales", *Fundación 1 de Mayo: Colección Estudios*, No 75, October 2013.

3. REFERENCES TO HUMAN DIGNITY IN THE TREATIES OF THE EUROPEAN UNION AND DERIVED LEGISLATION

In the Consolidated Version of the Treaty of the European Union 2012, the high contracting parties confirm in the preamble "their attachment to fundamental social rights as defined in the European Social Charter signed at Turin on 18 October 1961 and in the 1989 Community Charter of the Fundamental Social Rights of Workers".

Although it lacks binding legal effect, the 1989 Community Charter of Fundamental Social Rights of Workers establishes the principles on which European labour law is based. Several aspects of the work environment regulated by the Charter include the concept of dignity, the first of which is remuneration: the Charter establishes that all employment shall be fairly remunerated. To this end, in accordance with arrangements implemented in each country, workers shall be assured of an equitable wage, i.e. a wage sufficient to enable them to have "a decent standard of living". This phrase is used again to refer to the guaranteed resources that all workers, at the time of retirement, should be able to enjoy.

In Article 2 of the Treaty, it is established that "the Union is founded on the values of respect for human dignity, freedom, democracy, equality, the rule of law and the respect for human rights, including the rights of persons belonging to minorities. These values are common to the Member States in a society in which pluralism, non-discrimination, tolerance, justice, solidarity and equality between men and women prevail".

Therefore dignity is represented as a value in two ways: as the founding principle of the Union and as the common denominator for the Member States.

In the Consolidated Version of the Treaty on the Functioning of the European Union 2012, Title 1 of Part Three, referring to Union policies and internal actions, deals with the internal market, which comprises an area without internal borders in which the free movement of goods, persons, services and capital is ensured in accordance with the provisions of the Treaty (Article 26).

As for the definition of "goods", this is not found as such in the Treaty, having been defined by the Court of Justice of the European Union as "products which can be valued in money and which are capable, as such, of forming the subject of commercial transactions". However, Article 36 warns against prohibitions or restrictions on imports, exports or goods in transit on grounds of "public morality, public policy or public security, the protection of health and life of humans, animals or plants; the protection of national treasures possessing artistic, historic or archaeological value; or the protection of industrial and commercial property".

In fact, it should be noted that since 25 March 1957 the legal foundations of the Constitutional Treaty of the European Community were used to remove the barriers to a common market and this based on the free movement of goods and products with a view to adopting directives which in their turn resulted in the protection of safety and hygiene in the workplace, and therefore, of workers' health. The legal foundations of the Treaty destined to support the common market actually justified the adoption of laws, which, while establishing streamlined security requirements for products, eventually also amounted to an improvement of the health and safety of workers.[6]

The protection of persons, in particular of workers handling products or goods, has created a restriction on the freedom of trade, to the point of this being limited by principles of health protection and commercial unavailability, meaning that not all trading is legal.[7]

Regarding the free movement of persons, services and capital, the Treaty ensures the freedom of movement of workers within the Union (Article 45), the freedom of establishment (Article 49, including the right to take up and pursue activities as self-employed persons and to set up and manage undertakings), prohibiting all restrictions to this right. It also guarantees the freedom to provide services, i.e. services provided for remuneration. Accordingly, in Article 56 of the Treaty, all restrictions on this freedom are prohibited in respect of nationals of Member States who are established in a Member State other than that of the person for whom the services are intended. Finally, in Article 63, all restrictions on the movement of capital between Member States and between Member States and third countries are prohibited.

As we can see, no specific mention is made of dignity in these rules. However, it must be taken into account that this can be found in the laws stemming from these freedoms, especially in relation to the freedom of movement of workers within the Union.

Thus, in EU Regulation 492/2011 of the European Parliament and of the Council of 5 April 2011 on the freedom of movement of workers within the Union, the preamble states that in order for the right of freedom of movement to be exercised "by objective standards, in freedom and dignity", equality of treatment must be ensured legally and materially, with regard to all matters relating to the exercise of activities as self-employed persons and to eligibility for housing, and moreover that obstacles to the mobility of workers must be eliminated, in particular regarding the conditions for the integration of the worker's family into the host country. In this respect, we should not forget that reference is made to dignity in the preamble of Directive 2004/38/EC of the European Parliament and of the Council of 29 April 2004 on the right of the citizens of the Union and their family members to move and to reside freely within the territory of the Member States. It states that for every citizen of the

6 F. Camas Roda, *La normativa internacional y comunitaria de seguridad y salud en el trabajo*, Tirant lo Blanch, Valencia, 2003.

7 A. Supiot, *L'esprit de Philadelphie. La justice sociale face au marché total*, Paris, Seuil, 2010.

Union to have the right to move and reside freely within the territory of the Member States, "by objective standards, in freedom and dignity", this right must also be granted to family members, irrespective of nationality.

As a result, dignity becomes an objective condition for a person's right of freedom of movement. This means explicitly that in this freedom of movement, the fundamental right to human dignity, as laid down in Article 1 of the Charter, should not be viewed only in a negative way as a limitation or a deterrent, but that it has become a basic factor for another freedom to be exercised – that of the right of freedom of movement of workers, and consequently, of the right that accompanies it, as laid down in Article 15 of the Charter itself. This article regulates the freedom to choose an occupation and the right to engage in work (in the second part it states that "every citizen of the Union has the freedom to seek employment, to work, to exercise the right of establishment and to provide services in any Member State").

In this section, it is important to highlight that any derogation provided for in the legislation on the free movement of workers, particularly in relation to equal treatment with EU nationals, should be interpreted with restrictions due to its exceptional nature. Directive 2004/38/EC offers Member States the possibility of refusing to grant welfare benefits or maintenance support to people making use of the freedom of movement. The judgment of the Court of 11 November 2014 in Case C-333/13, *Dano v. Jobcenter Leipzig* authorized this refusal of the request for social welfare benefits by a Community citizen who lacked economic resources and had not been in employment. This judgment fails to evaluate what obtaining these benefits represents for the citizen's dignity in relation to the freedom of movement of workers (a freedom which, in the light of this judgment, would not have been denied if the citizen had been seeking employment). In any event, the question of dignity must also play a part in cases of free movement, and more so in situations of differentiation or discrimination regarding requests for social benefits by non-nationals. Nonetheless, we must emphasize the need to preserve the exceptional nature of any obstacle to the freedom of movement, the pursuit of equal treatment for European citizens in the exercise of that freedom and the refusal to automatically favour financial or budgetary interests over and above social concerns.

Apart from the previously mentioned references in Regulation 492 and the 2004 Directive, there are literally no other explicit links between the freedoms laid down in the Treaty or the rights set out in the Charter and human dignity.

Still, some authors defend these links based on the definition of certain rights in international law. Thus, for example, the Universal Declaration of Human Rights recognizes the right to just and favourable remuneration guaranteeing the worker and his or her family a decent existence. Dignity is used here as a guiding parameter for public authorities when regulating the right to just remuneration. Consequently, there should be a positive dimension to the right to human dignity which links it to the provision of a minimum living wage, or decent means of subsistence in the European Union, a matter which, nevertheless, has not been incorporated into EU primary law.[8]

4. HUMAN DIGNITY AS AN INTEGRATED, TRANSVERSAL ASSUMPTION

4.1. THE EFFECTS OF DIGNITY IN RELATION TO WORK

I have referred to the fact that in the preamble of the Charter human dignity is a value cherished by the Union, which on establishing European Union citizenship "places the individual at the heart of its activities". This fact should induce us to consider the conditions under which the aforementioned human dignity is respected in one of its areas of vital importance: work. When we place the individual at the centre of Union protection we cannot ignore his or her dignity regarding work.

It should not be forgotten that the Declaration of Philadelphia of 1944, concerning the aims and purposes of the International Labour Organization, reaffirms the fundamental principle that "labour is not a commodity". The value of human dignity should make it impossible for a person to be reduced to a mere object or commodity in work-related actions. The concept of dignity has converted labour rights into human rights in the workplace, as a result of which workers have to be treated with the necessary respect and are governed by rights with full legislative power in the work environment.[9]

This has actually been the role of labour law in that it represents the way in which the right to human dignity in the workplace has materialized, and this despite its focus on wage and salaried workers with an employment contract. However, the scope of this protective legislation should be extended to other categories, such as self-employed workers.[10]

To make human dignity in the workplace a reality, labour law underwent a process of constitutionalization in the Member States of the European Union in which its social character was strengthened. On the basis of this, the public authorities, and in particular the legislator, are obliged to pass laws and promote political action aimed at facilitating the creation of not just any work but, in the words of the ILO, of "decent" or dignified work. This means productive work in conditions of freedom, equity, human security and dignity, thus offering better

---

8 P. Serna, "Dignidad humana", in: E. Álvarez Conde and V. Garrido Mayol, *Comentarios a la Constitución Europea*, Libro II, Tirant lo Blanch, 2004, pp. 191–240.

9 C. Chacartegui Jávega, *Dignidad de los trabajadores y derechos humanos del trabajo según la jurisprudencia del Tribunal Europeo de Derechos Humanos*, Ed. Bomarzo, Albacete, 2013.

10 M. Rigaux, *Droit du travail ou droit de la concurrence sociale?. Essai sur un droit de la dignité de l'Homme au travail (re)mis en cause*, Bruylant, 2009.

prospects for the workers' personal development and respect for their dignity, and this within a legal framework that recognizes and actively defends the workers' rights and gives them access to adequate social protection.[11]

4.2. A THREAT TO LABOUR LAW: THE DEVALUATION OF WORK

The prevailing arguments in favour of the reforms are that labour law is accountable for the financial crisis, even though this is far from the truth. Instead, the crisis was caused by non-work-related factors of a financial, economic and political nature. In fact, the effects of the crisis on the labour market, for example, in terms of job destruction and increased unemployment, should not be attributed to labour law. Employment contracts or measures to facilitate dismissals may vary according to specific labour legislation regulations, but they are the tools and not the causes of the employment crisis. The real causes are, amongst others, business decisions to downsize or close down companies faced with difficulties in the current economic setting, the credit crunch, bank bailouts, the drop in domestic demand and fiscal adjustments.[12]

Nonetheless, holding labour law accountable has meant its mission has been reshaped, giving it a basically economic purpose. As a result, over and above labour law's function of promoting a balance between the interests of employers and employees, which was its basis, a shift has occurred in which competitiveness and business viability have been given priority in order to create jobs. This has been carried out by reformulating labour legislation in such a way that the individual rights of employees have been reduced and more power has been granted to the employer while at the same time reducing the collective bargaining power of workers' representatives.

Given that there are still high levels of unemployment, and more importantly that the employment created is characterized by highly precarious working conditions, it should be clear that the labour law reforms have not yielded the expected results.

In fact, the most obvious result of this reform process is that employment has lost its basic function of guaranteeing a decent existence; the reduction in labour rights in the workplace at the same time as an increase in power for employers

11 F. Valdes Dal-Ré, Voto particular que formula a la Sentencia 8/2015 del Tribunal Constitucional de 22 de enero de 2015 dictada en el recurso de inconstitucionalidad núm. 5603-2012, al que se adhieren la Magistrada Doña Adela Asua Batarrita y el Magistrado Don Luis Ignacio Ortega Álvarez.

12 M.E. Casas Baamonde, "La eficacia y la eficiencia del Derecho del Trabajo: reflexiones sobre un Derecho cuestionado por la economía y el desempleo", *Relaciones Laborales*, No 30, Sección Doctrina, Octubre 2014, Año 30, Editorial La Ley: La Ley 6289/2014.

in labour relations, means, in practice, that the effectiveness of the fundamental rights of workers within the company has been reduced.

Added to this is the phenomenon of the gradual reduction in workers' wages, a factor that may also affect their dignity. To take one example, the wage reduction carried out in Spain in the context of the labour market reforms, and the resulting economic uncertainty, have led to an increase in poverty. It should also be noted that the pleas of the Spanish trade unions before the European Committee of Social Rights, in particular on the failure to comply with Article 4 of the Charter (right to fair remuneration), as a result of the Spanish labour law reforms, state: "This is a situation which not only has changed but has reduced the ability of the minimum wage to ensure a decent standard of living for working people and their families [...] At its current levels, the MLW (minimum living wage) is bordering on the poverty line in homes with just one member and is clearly below that level in homes comprising at least two people."[13]

The possibility that the job carried out by the worker fails to cover his or her basic needs is a symptom of the collapse of labour law, one of whose basic objectives is precisely to ensure that work is a key to achieving financial security.[14] However, even though appropriate remuneration for work is a key element in achieving a decent standard of living, decent employment requires more than that, more specifically quality criteria. The concept of decent work implies a remuneration which ensures quality of life in combination with a quality job, governed by criteria such as job security and decent working conditions in terms of working hours, work–life balance and health and safety in the workplace.

In short, if a worker is subject to precarious working conditions and remuneration that cannot guarantee a decent existence, the basic principles of dignity are violated.

To address this situation from a legal standpoint, the following proposals may be considered.

Firstly, labour market reforms are affecting the Member States of the European Union at different rates. Although these reforms have been enforced by European institutions, all countries have focused on what is taking place in their corresponding labour legislation. This is the so-called "re-nationalization" effect that underlies labour law thinking.[15]

---

13 CCOO-UGT, *Alegaciones de las Confederaciones sindicales de Comisiones Obreras y la Unión General de Trabajadoes al 26e. Informe presetntado por el Gobierno de España al Comité Europea de Derechos Sociales, sobre el cumplimiento de la Carta Social Europea*, 23 July 2014.

14 A. Supiot, *Que sais-je? Le Droit du travail*, Puf, 2004.

15 M.E. Casas Baamonde, "La eficacia y la eficiencia del Derecho del Trabajo: reflexiones sobre un Derecho cuestionado por la economía y el desempleo", *Relaciones Laborales*, No 30, Sección Doctrina, Octubre 2014, Año 30, Editorial La Ley: La Ley 6289/2014.

In the light of this, international labour regulations that lay down minimum requirements for work – ILO's "decent work" – and the international instruments of the Council of Europe and the United Nations regarding human rights, transnational collective agreements and non-work-related international pacts and agreements which include social and labour values, would be the only useful tools to curb the more negative consequences of offshoring and business absorption (real humanitarian catastrophes and environmental disasters).[16] The laws laid down in international human rights documents and their universal standards of protection are not indisputable, especially without international monitoring agencies able to control non-compliance by States and those private organizations and institutions which are free from any control, but whose actions affect the human rights of the individuals or groups concerned, especially their so-called social and cultural rights.

Therefore, the defence of the values inherent to European labour law and, consequently, the protection of workers' dignity must inevitably involve regulations stemming from European social law, rather than from national laws. The conclusion we can draw is that the continued existence of labour law in the light of its founding principles, and the constitutional recognition of the workers' protection, is dependent on European social law, and above all, on the values currently in force in the EU's Charter and Treaties.

Secondly, the main charge against an economy-focused motivation underlying labour law is that it has led to a reformulation of its institutions. In relation to the labour market reforms carried out in Spain, for example, new employment contracts have been concluded with long probationary periods during which the employer is free to take unilateral decisions on the worker's continuity. Similarly, it has become easier for employers to take decisions that affect working hours and pay cuts laid down in the employment contract, and even to terminate the contract itself. More specifically, employers have been given an advantage with regard to collective bargaining with the workers' representatives, enabling them, amongst other things, to downgrade the workers' working conditions at the end of the period of an agreement, if there is not another agreement to replace it. Preference is also given to company agreements, in which the influence of the workers' representatives plays a lesser role, compared to collective agreements at a sector-based or supra-company level, in which trade unions exert greater pressure. Finally, the employer may also downgrade the working conditions set out in certain collective agreements, thus affecting the binding force of these agreements for the workers.

In order to analyse the validity of these labour market reforms, the legal actors have used the dogmatic concepts integrated in the labour laws that

---

16 M.E. Casas Baamonde, "La eficacia y la eficiencia del Derecho del Trabajo: reflexiones sobre un Derecho cuestionado por la economía y el desempleo", *Relaciones Laborales*, No 30, Sección Doctrina, Octubre 2014, Año 30, Editorial La Ley: La Ley 6289/2014.

underwent changes following the new labour legislation as filters to see how they adapt to the values derived from labour law and to the basic principles and rights laid down in the Spanish Constitution. For example, the evaluation of a violation of labour law in contracts with excessively long probationary periods is based on what a probationary period actually means. Similarly, assessing the possibility for the employer to downgrade working conditions laid down in a collective agreement no longer in force is based on the scope of the actual legal regulations that govern these agreements. This clash in the legal procedure of the new labour institutions has not taken into account whether the new labour laws on workers' rights have affected the workers' dignity, or put another way, whether establishing an excessively long probationary period with greater powers for the employer to freely terminate the contract may actually undermine the workers' dignity.

Accordingly, the legal actors should adjust the laws derived from labour market reforms in Europe in relation to the right to human dignity. Dignity, understood as a value from which fundamental rights are derived, is a legal concept which should be used to evaluate whether the fundamental labour laws (affecting contracts, dismissals, collective bargaining), which are being passed with the sole purpose of favouring competitiveness and business viability, can come under the protection of its "umbrella".

Thirdly, dignity is an intrinsic part of the economic liberties laid down in the constitutional treaties of the European Union. Therefore, these liberties should be exercised in this vein.

As mentioned before, dignity is addressed explicitly in relation to the freedom of movement of workers in the European Union. However, this does not happen in the case of economy-focused liberties which form the basis of the internal market, free movement of goods, services and capital, guaranteed in this case by the constitutional treaties.

Still, we have seen that, in the exercise of these freedoms, for example regarding the free movement of goods, the need to preserve certain goods directly related to the integrity and health of persons and workers has not been ignored; in the words of the Treaty, public policy, public morality and public security or protection of health and life.

In fact, underpinning these issues is the dignity of the workers themselves, not only as subjects of these liberties but also in exercising them. As Supiot said, the freedom of movement of goods and capital is not an aim in itself; its true worth is the way in which it is actually used: to improve the workers' lot.[17]

Accordingly, we need to transfer to the workplace the judgment of the European Court of Justice of 14 October in Case C-36/02, *Omega Spielhallen v. Oberbürgermeisterin der Bundesstadt Bonn*, in which the compatibility of human dignity with the freedom to "provide services" and the free "movement

17 A. Supiot, *L'esprit de Philadelphie. La justice sociale face au marché total*, Paris, Seuil, 2010.

of goods" was condemned regarding a game called "Playing at killing", whose commercial exploitation was banned by the German national authorities because it simulated killing and the trivialization of violence, and constituted an affront to the fundamental values of the community (human dignity).

The Court of Justice stated that "the prohibition of the commercial exploitation of games involving the simulation of acts of violence against persons, in particular the representation of acts of homicide, corresponds to the level of protection of human dignity, which the national constitution (Germany) seeks to guarantee [... and] by prohibiting only the variant of the laser game whose object is to fire on human targets and thus 'play at killing' persons. The German authorities' decision to ban the game] does not go beyond what is necessary in order to attain the objective pursued [and] cannot be regarded as a measure that unjustifiably undermines the freedom to provide services".[18]

5. CONCLUSIONS

In this contribution, I have set out to demonstrate that human dignity is destined to play a key role in protecting workers in the light of the scope of the reforms being carried out in labour law.

With this aim in mind, I have listed the references to dignity in European social law, the implementation of which should prevail over domestic labour laws adopted by EU Member States. In addition, I have shown how the labour market reforms taking place in Europe are devaluing work, leading to situations which do not ensure a decent standard of living for the workers. What is more, labour law itself is being questioned. One of its main functions is to establish the value of workers' dignity in the area of labour relations.

On the other hand, this contribution also seeks a way to promote the use of the values and rights integrated in European legislation as guardians of the inherent traits of labour law. Accordingly, the references to human dignity contained in European social law must be used as concepts to fight the social consequences which the labour market reforms are causing. Indeed, dignity should be used as a legal instrument in the interpretation of the labour laws that are being drafted in the European Union and, therefore, in the fight against the precariousness of working conditions and deprivation of workers' rights.

Furthermore, it should not be forgotten, as mentioned in the last part of this contribution, that even the economic freedoms laid down in the founding

---

18 A. Tapia Hermida, "La protección de los Derechos Fundamentales en el Derecho comunitario. Sus funciones. La 'Dignidad humana' como principio general del Derecho y norma jurídica", *Estudios Financieros*, No 21/2005.

Treaties of the European Union are also based on respect for human dignity and, therefore, cannot be implemented while ignoring workers' fundamental rights in the workplace.

PART II

TESTIMONIES FROM THE FIELD

CHAPTER 9
THE NATIONAL LEGAL BATTLE AGAINST SOCIAL EXPLOITATION IN AUSTRIA

Walter Gagawczuk*

1. THE WAGE SYSTEM IN AUSTRIA

There is no general minimum wage laid down in Austrian law. Wages are usually regulated by collective agreements at industry level. The negotiations normally take place between the unions and the Chamber of Commerce. Because membership of the Chamber of Commerce is compulsory for employers, the collective agreements cover all employers. They also cover all trade union members and all employees (the so-called *Außenseiterwirkung* [non-member effect], §12 *Arbeitsverfassungsgesetz*). Consequently, the collective agreements have a very broad range of application, covering about 96% of the workforce.

Information about wages is available at: www.kollektivvertrag.at. At the moment, the site can only be consulted in German, but the most important information should also be available in English in the near future.

The wages stipulated by the collective agreements also apply to employees who are working for non-Austrian employers and who are posted in Austria from other countries. This means that these employees are entitled to the same wage that has been determined by collective agreement and that is paid to comparative employees by comparative employers at the place of employment (principle of "equal pay for equal work in the same place"; §§7, 7a, 7b *Arbeitsvertragsrechts-Anpassungsgesetz*).

Until May 2011, only civil law covered this for these employees. For instance, a posted iron bender from Slovakia who only received a wage for his work in Austria under Slovakian provisions could sue for the difference in accordance with the Austrian collective agreement for the building and construction

* Chamber of Labour, Vienna.

industry. However, for various reasons, this hardly ever happened in practice. It became clear that the option of making a claim under civil law was not suited for enforcement of these rights. Therefore, the worker representatives requested that Austria set up an official control mechanism with the ability to impose sanctions if the wages provided for are not paid.

2. THE ANTI-WAGE AND SOCIAL DUMPING ACT

Since May 2011 a new law has been in force against wage dumping. It is called the Anti-Wage and Social Dumping Act. It includes an official control mechanism for the wages provided for. This mechanism does not only apply to posted workers but to all workers. This means that if a domestic employer underpays his workers, he too can expect sanctions.

The penalties range between €1,000 and €10,000 for each employee. If the wage dumping affects more than three workers, the range of penalties per employee is automatically increased. In that case, it lies between €2,000 and €20,000 per employee, and between €4,000 and €50,000 in the case of repeated infringement. For example, if a construction company tries to obtain a competitive advantage over its competitors by not paying the wages provided for by the collective agreement and if inspectors find that wage dumping has taken place on the building site for five workers, the employer's minimum penalty amounts to €10,000 (2,000 x 5) and the maximum penalty to €100,000. In the event of repeated infringement, the minimum penalty is €20,000, with a maximum of €250,000. The employer may also expect his trade licence to be withdrawn or – in the case of a foreign employer – may be banned from working in Austria for at least one year.

However, if the wage is only slightly below the collectively agreed minimum wage or if the employer has only slightly infringed the rules, and if the employer has paid the employee the difference, no complaint should be filed.

Imposing administrative fines on foreign employers, however, is difficult, sometimes even impossible. Perhaps this will change once the Member States have implemented Enforcement Directive 2014/67/EU (the directive should be transposed by 18 June 2016 at the latest). However, until there is effective cross-border enforcement of administrative penalties, there is a specific provision to make sure that the penalties are paid. Foreign employees who provide their services in Austria, such as people working on building projects for temporary employment agencies, people who provide cleaning services, or who drive a van, etc., have an Austrian client and are entitled to the wage or the temporary employment fee (in the case of temporary employment agencies) that is laid down by Austrian law. The authorities can refer to this provision in order to ensure the enforcement of administrative penalties if wage dumping is suspected. In most cases, enforcing the fine abroad will no longer be necessary.

3. APPLICABLE LAW FOR CROSS-BORDER EMPLOYMENT IN THE TRANSPORT SECTOR

While there is a rather clear legal situation in the construction sector as to which law is applicable, there is – at least to some degree – uncertainty in the transport sector.

Since the judgment of the European Court of Justice in cases C-29/10 *Koelzsch* and C-384/10 *Voogsgeerd*, there has been more clarity regarding the application of the Rome I Regulation, particularly as regards the meaning of "habitual place of work" (Article 8(2)) in the transport sector.

As to the Posting of Workers Directive, it is quite clear that it is applicable in cases of cabotage, but there is great uncertainty in other cases (bilateral transport, transit). In order to illuminate this question, the Austrian Chamber of Labour commissioned Prof. Dr Michaela Windisch-Graetz from the University of Vienna to write a study on this. The main results of this study are described below.

For posting situations that do not fall within the special conflict of laws scope of the Posting of Workers Directive 96/71/EC, the general conflict of laws regulations of Regulation 593/2008/EC (Rome I Regulation) are applicable. The Rome I Regulation and the Posting of Workers Directive jointly and conclusively regulate the conflict of laws rules.

Fundamentally, the employment law of the habitual place of work is applicable to workers in the transport industry. In order to establish the habitual place of work, it is necessary to determine from which country the employee starts the transport journeys, from which country instructions on these trips are received and from where the work is organized, along with where the work equipment is located. It must also be verified where the goods are mainly transported to, where they are unloaded and where the employee returns to after his journeys.

The Posting of Workers Directive (PWD) contains special regulations in the event that the conflict of laws judgment based on the Rome I Regulation results in the habitual place of work not being located in the host State.

A systematic interpretation of the PWD is suggestive of the will of the European legislators to include the transport industry within the scope of the Posting of Workers Directive too. The competency provisions of the TFEU concerning transport services do not preclude this.

The PWD authorizes Member States to extend their collective labour agreements to posted workers in areas other than the construction industry, provided that this is compatible with the TFEU, particularly with regard to the fundamental freedoms.

Within this context, the scope of the PWD and especially Article 1(3) have to be considered:

> "This Directive shall apply to the extent that the undertakings referred to in paragraph 1 take one of the following transnational measures:
>
> (a) post workers to the territory of a Member State on their account and under their direction, under a contract concluded between the undertaking making the posting and the party for whom the services are intended, operating in that Member State, provided there is an employment relationship between the undertaking making the posting and the worker during the period of posting; or
> (b) post workers to an establishment or to an undertaking owned by the group in the territory of a Member State, provided there is an employment relationship between the undertaking making the posting and the worker during the period of posting; or
> (c) being a temporary employment undertaking or placement agency, hire out a worker to a user undertaking established or operating in the territory of a Member State, provided there is an employment relationship between the temporary employment undertaking or placement agency and the worker during the period of posting."

The most important case in the transport sector is found in section (a).

Consider the following example. A client ("party for whom the services are intended") in Salzburg (Austria) orders ("under a contract") a company in Budapest (Hungary) to bring some goods from Budapest to Salzburg. The company in Hungary posts an employee to Austria to deliver the goods.

The PWD applies (Article 1(3)(a)). For the duration of the posted employee's working time in Austria, the Austrian terms and conditions of employment regarding Article 3 of the PWD apply as long as they are better than the Hungarian terms and conditions of employment.

To summarize, this means that the scope of the Posting of Workers Directive includes the transport industry. Only in some cases the posting requirements of the Posting of Workers Directive (Article 1) are not fulfilled because the transport undertaking that posts workers to another Member State did not conclude a contract with a recipient party that operates in the host Member State (especially in the transit transport industry). As a result, Article 1(3)(b) (posting within the group) or (c) (posting of temporary worker) is not applicable.

CHAPTER 10
FIGHTING THE GREY ECONOMY WITH NATIONAL LEGISLATION
The Case of Finland

Heini Polamo*

1. INTRODUCTION

When the Finnish government embarked on a battle against the grey economy in 2011, commercial goods transport was defined as one of the focus areas. This reflected in Finland's revised *Act on Commercial Haulage of Goods by Road* (21.7.2006/693), which came into force in two phases in 2013 and 2014. Customer liability was introduced in the first phase.

Since 25 April 2013, Finnish customers of haulage companies are obliged, before concluding a transport contract, to verify that for example:

- the haulier has a current licence for freight transport on public roads or; the right to carry freight without a licence;
- when the contract price is liable to VAT, that the haulier is registered for VAT;
- in cabotage, that the company carrying out the haulage work has the right to engage in cabotage; and
- the haulier is fulfilling his legal obligations as an employer.

A particularly low price for transport services may indicate that the haulier is not fulfilling his legal obligations and should give the customer reason to suspect negligence. If in such cases the customer fails to conduct proper checks before signing a haulage contract, he will be breaking the law and may be subject to a fine (32 §). These measures can be considered stricter than general contractor's liability.

* Finnish Transport and Logistics SKAL.

In order to speed up efficient implementation of these measures, Finnish Transport and Logistics SKAL has written and distributed two guidebooks for professional purchasers in cooperation with the Finnish authorities. These guidebooks present practical examples of the revised law and list sources for checking information related to customer liability. For example, the Finnish authorities maintain open-to-all online registers for checking Community licences and VAT information.

2. COMMERCIAL GOODS TRANSPORT AND GREY ECONOMY IN FINLAND

Commercial goods transport on Finnish roads concerns some 9,000 road haulage operators with an annual turnover of over €5 billion. The financial impact of the grey economy is approximately €500 million. It includes, among others, unlicensed commercial goods transport, engaging in illegal cabotage and failing to comply with legal obligations, such as offering appropriate wages, paying taxes and having the required insurance. Phenomena related to social dumping fall into these categories. Another element in the grey economy are the so-called "serial" entrepreneurs who cut their prices to generate cash quickly, deliberately neglect their legal obligations, go bankrupt so that other parties have to pay the costs, and then start up new haulage businesses using new trading names.

In the SKAL Transport Barometer Survey of June 2014, which had 554 respondents, unfair competition comprising various forms of grey economy was considered a major challenge by 61% of Finnish haulage operators. The Finnish administration does not provide official records of foreign goods transport or cabotage. According to SKAL's own traffic calculation conducted on major roads across Finland in 2012, some 8% of commercial goods transport vehicles carry foreign registration plates.

3. FINNISH HAULIERS SUPPORT STRONG MEASURES TO FIGHT THE GREY ECONOMY

One of the results of the revised law was that at the end of 2013, the Finnish Grey Economy Investigation Unit investigated the amount of tax owed by transport operators. More than 1,000 companies owed amounts exceeding €12,000. These debts had to be settled by July 2014. As a direct consequence, about 300 transport operators had their operating licences cancelled. In SKAL's Transport Barometer of September 2014, 92% of 677 respondents supported the investigation and 83% considered licence cancellation an acceptable penalty for failing to meet tax liabilities.

Finnish Customs is currently investigating a total of 35 cases involving customer liability, most of which concern unlicensed transport or illegal cabotage in conjunction with negligence of customer liability.

CHAPTER 11

THE NATIONAL LEGAL BATTLE AGAINST SOCIAL EXPLOITATION

National Practices of Finnish Labour Inspection

Jarno VIRTANEN*

There are several public inspection authorities operating in the field of road transport in Finland. The Centre for Economic Development, Transport and the Environment is the competent authority for market access. It grants for example community licences and driver attestations. Police and Customs are responsible for roadside checks. They also control road safety, cabotage transport and social legislation relating to driving times and rest periods.

The Occupational Safety and Health Administration (Labour Inspection) oversees labour law as a whole, including the posting of workers and the health and safety provisions. It also carries out company checks to ensure that the social legislation relating to driving times is respected. Apart from that, labour inspectors also oversee the contractor's obligations which apply to all fields of business. As a whole, there are over 370 labour inspectors working in the field. In 2014, they carried out 25,000 work site inspections, over 1,000 of which were focused on the road transport industry in one way or another.

Labour inspections focus on actions that limit the grey economy and promote longer working careers. The concept of the grey economy also covers aspects of social dumping. Part of the problem of the grey economy is the failure to comply with the rules of the labour market. The grey economy is a serious social phenomenon that can only be successfully prevented if public authorities cooperate with each other. Labour inspections are one part of the comprehensive battle against the grey economy.

Labour Inspectorates check in particular whether employers only hire employees who have the right to work in Finland, whether the conditions of

* Ministry of Social Affairs and Health, Finland.

employment comply with the law and whether subcontractors have carried out their social obligations. Monitoring health and safety regulations is also part of the fight against the grey economy. Indeed, undue financial benefit may be gained if health and safety regulations are deliberately ignored.

Labour inspectors can only impose administrative measures. If shortcomings are noticed at the workplace, the inspector can issue a written recommendation or an improvement notice. An improvement notice may be issued only in specific situations and it can lead to a binding administrative decision. Particularly when it comes to matters of labour law, written advice is the only way to remedy an illegal situation. The Labour Inspectorate cannot impose a fine of a penal nature or another punishment. However, Labour Inspectorates can notify the police of cases where there are probable grounds to suspect that a crime has been committed. Therefore, correction of some inadequacies regarding labour law, for example underpayment, is limited to administrative guidance. Only cases of severe underpayment can be notified to the police. However, the Finnish Act on the Contractor's Obligations and Liability provides for an administrative negligence fee that can be ordered by the Labour Inspectorate if the contractor has neglected his obligation to check the background of the contracting partner before conclusion of the contract. The abovementioned Contractor's Liability Act differs from the Act on Commercial Haulage of Goods by Road which provides for specific customer liability.

In 2014, the Labour Inspectorates started a nationwide project called "Tackling grey economy in road transport". Within the framework of this project, all inspections have the same agenda and they are carried out in the same manner in order to achieve comparable statistics and a snapshot for future inspection needs. The choice of inspection targets is vital: the inspectors use a risk rating system and use information from other public authorities as well as from employer and employee associations.

During the road transport project, the inspectors have already built close and personal connections with the transport licence authorities and the police. Information from company checks is sent to the police and vice versa. The provision of information from labour inspections to the transport licence authorities appears to be an effective way to prevent the grey economy since the transport licence can be cancelled in the case of the most severe breaches.

Effective prevention of the grey economy requires a lot of expertise, time and resources from labour inspectors. With limited resources, it is essential that inspections focus on the correct targets instead of on a large number of inspections. Cooperation between public authorities and social partners is the way forward.